Minka and Margaret

Minka and Margaret

The heroic story of two
nurses captured in the jungle

by

PHYLLIS THOMPSON

OMF BOOKS

© OVERSEAS MISSIONARY FELLOWSHIP

First published jointly by Hodder and Stoughton Ltd and Overseas Missionary Fellowship, 1976
This edition 1978

An extract from 'Let the Earth Hear His Voice' is reproduced by permission of the Billy Graham Evangelistic Association.

ISBN 0 85363 121 2

Published by the Overseas Missionary Fellowship, Belmont, The Vine, Sevenoaks, Kent, TN13 3TZ, and printed and bound in Great Britain at The Camelot Press Ltd, Southampton

The sovereign operation of the Holy Spirit in our lives over these days may and almost certainly will involve unexpected and costly demands. What price am I, what price are you prepared to pay? Do you recall the words of Thomas when he said, 'Except I shall see in his hands the print of the nails, I will not believe'? There is a sense in which the world is saying the same thing. Is there the equivalent of the print of the nails in my hands, in yours, or are our hands soft and clean because they have never grappled with sin and suffering?

BISHOP A. J. DAIN, International Congress on World Evangelisation (*Let the Earth Hear His Voice*, Worldwide Publications, page 15).

CONTENTS

CONTENTS

PROLOGUE

'Two women missionaries kidnapped by bandits!'
'Welsh nurse and Dutch companion abducted in South Thailand!'
'Malay terrorists capture missionary nurses!'

It was 23rd April, 1974. In one of the remotest areas of the ancient Asian kingdom of Thailand Miss Margaret Morgan from Britain and Miss Minka Hanskamp from Holland, while attending to leprosy patients in a rural clinic, had been taken off at gun point by four men. They had been driven off in a green Mazda taxi. One of the men had been heard to say the nurses were being taken to tend some sick people. They were believed to have been heading for a bandit hide-out in the jungle.

Kidnappings, murders, hold-ups and gun battles between the military police and the bandits had been going on for years in the troubled provinces on the Malaysian border, but this was the first time western missionaries had been abducted, and it was NEWS. Telegraph wires crackled, telephone bells rang, staccato radio messages darted from country to country.

'The abducted women are members of the Overseas Missionary Fellowship. Head office in Thailand in Bangkok. International headquarters in Singapore. Get the story . . . Get photographs . . .'

The news media acted so quickly that the Embassies and the OMF were hard put to it to keep a step ahead and notify the relatives and those most intimately concerned before they heard it over the radio or saw news flashes on the TV. When Ian Murray, Superintendent of the OMF work in South Thailand, received the first indication of the kidnapping through the local police, he went off to confirm the report, then phoned the OMF office in Bangkok. He had difficulty in getting through, and when he did so he learned the news had already reached there. 'It's in the early evening papers here,' he was told. Then came the anxious question:

'How bad is it?'

Ian Murray was fairly optimistic. 'I think they'll let the girls go after a day or two,' he said. 'There was a big gun battle not far away a couple of nights ago, and they've probably been taken off to tend the wounded. Not likely to keep them after that. Better cable Singapore and London, though.'

Bangkok time was six hours ahead of London so it was early afternoon when the cable arrived in London, about the same time as a telephone call was received from the Foreign Office. A few minutes later the telephone rang in a terraced house in a narrow street in Porth, gateway to the Rhondda valleys of South Wales.

Mrs Morgan had just finished washing up the dinner things, and walked through the sunny back room to the front passage where the telephone stood on a small table. She picked up the receiver.

'Is that Mrs Morgan?' a man's voice asked. 'I'm phoning from London, from the OMF. This is Norman Pateman speaking.' He paused a moment, then went on, 'It's about Margaret. We've had some rather bad news, I'm afraid.'

She caught her breath. She'd known Margaret wasn't well. Her weekly letters had come as usual, cheerful and full of news, but each one recently had made passing references to a severe headache . . . an allergy . . . an attack of diarrhoea . . . Margaret was ill! That's why they were phoning from London.

'I've been expecting this,' she said, trying to keep her voice calm.

'You've been expecting it?' was the surprised reply. 'What have you been expecting?'

'She's ill, isn't she? I could tell from her letters. Is it serious?'

'No, it isn't that. It's worse, I'm afraid . . .'

'Worse!' What did he mean?

'She's been captured by bandits. We've just received a cable from Bangkok. I'll read it to you. *Morgan Hanskamp taken by bandits. Murray hopeful early release. Presume taken to care for wounded.*'

'We can be thankful she's not alone,' the voice continued gently. 'There seems good reason to hope they'll be released soon. We'll be praying very earnestly. And of course we'll keep in close touch with you. When we get any further news we'll let you know at once . . .'

But she scarcely heard what he was saying. Her mind seemed to have come to a standstill at those words, 'captured by bandits'. So this was it. She'd been conscious something was going to happen, but she'd thought it was to do with Margaret's health. This was worse. Captured by bandits—what would they do to her? Where had they taken her?

She stood irresolute after she'd put down the receiver, wondering what to do. It was no use phoning Elaine. She wouldn't be back from work yet. Whom could she tell? Who was there to feel as she felt, as Elaine would feel when she heard her sister had been taken by bandits?

She thought of Bert. Bert and Alma. They'd known Margaret since she was a little girl, loved her as they might have loved a younger sister, had shared with her the problems and perplexities as well as the joys and encouragements of the pastoral work of the church. When Margaret had been home on her last furlough she'd gone out soon after breakfast nearly every morning, walking briskly along the narrow pavement to the station approach, then round the corner and into the back door that led into the church premises, to have a talk and prayer with Bert. It had been part of the day's routine, just as any afternoon she was free she went for a walk with Alma, climbing up the steep hillside over-looking the narrow valley in which the sturdy grey stone rows of houses that had been built for the miners looked like boulders in a dried-up river bed. There was no-one in Porth who would receive the shock that had come to her more deeply than the Taylors.

Mrs Morgan picked up the receiver again and dialled their number.

'I'll be round immediately,' Mr Taylor said as soon as he heard, and within fifteen minutes he had parked his car in an empty space overlooking the railway line and was hurry-ing along Taff Street, passing a door and a window, a door and a window, all along the narrow pavement until he came to number 35. Here the front door stood open, ready to receive him, and he entered, hands outstretched. 'Gwyneth!' he said, grasping hers. Words seemed inadequate, trivial.

They sat down, and she related again the message that had come over the phone.

'I can't come to the prayer meeting this evening,' she said. 'I must stay in. There might be another phone call. There might be some more news.'

'Of course,' he said. 'I'm staying right here with you, and Alma's coming when I go off to the meeting. We'll *pray*. God will be with her . . . He *is* with her . . . That this news should have come today—prayer meeting day. Margaret will know we're all praying for her. She'll remember it's Tuesday. God will hear our prayers! She'll be released soon. Why, by this time next week we may be having a praise meeting!' He spoke confidently, and Mrs Morgan nodded. She wanted to share his confidence, but she still felt be-numbed. She was listening for the telephone. It might ring again.

In Holland a message from London had been delivered at the home of the OMF representative, Sonja van den Bergh. Could she break the news to Mrs Hanskamp that her daughter had been kidnapped by bandits? Assure Mrs Hanskamp of our earnest prayers . . .

The vigil had begun.

CHAPTER ONE

GOD CHOSE WHAT IS WEAK

From Margaret Morgan's notebook

See the waves, My child?
They are like My compassion
Compassion for those who are
    sad, lonely, troubled and sick.
The waves never cease,
They come again and again.
My compassion is like this
    flowing out constantly
    to My children and
    to those who are lost.

I want to share something of this with you, My child,
    and cause the waves of My compassion to roll within your soul.
That you may understand a little of how I feel,
    of how I love,
    of the concern I have.

Trust Me, My child,
I tell you this yet again,
Trust Me to minister
To minister to yourself
    and to others through you.
Keep close to Me, is all I ask.
Be open and ready to receive My fullness.
I would use you as a channel
A channel of My compassion
    of My love and grace.
                        M.M.

While on holiday by the sea.

From the point of view of human selection Margaret Morgan would have been a most unlikely choice for the self-denying, often distasteful work of a leprosy worker in a tropical country. That the final appointment of her forty years of life should be martyrdom as a captive in the jungle would have been inconceivable to those who knew her as a delicate little only child who caught cold easily, and frequently had digestive troubles. There was a fastidiousness about her too, increasingly noticeable as she grew into her teens, which indicated that if she followed her natural inclinations she would live in surroundings as well ordered and artistic as she could make them, that her table would charm the eye with its dainty china and gleaming cutlery, and that she would have plenty of time to listen to classical music though little or none for pursuits demanding study and the application of the mind. She was gentle and quiet, unmalicious and sunny-tempered, but she gave little evidence of possessing the calibre commonly associated with martyrs. But, as the Apostle Paul had observed, it is from among such people that God makes His choices.

She was born in the Welsh mining village of Porth on 15th June, 1934, at a time when the coal mining industry was on the downgrade, with the threat of collieries closing, and queues of men, caps over eyes, shoulders hunched, lining up day after day, waiting without much hope for a job in the pits. There was a greyness about the villages in those days, the greyness of poverty, and her father was thankful for a steady, if poorly-paid job. As debt and rent collector in a chain grocery firm, he knew his way up and down, in and out of the rows of sturdy little houses that lined the steep, winding valleys of the Rhondda. He lived in one of them himself, up on one of the terraces overlooking the railway, not far from the chapel where he was one of the elders. From a very early age his little daughter was taken there, and although throughout her whole life Margaret was a loyal, enthusiastic member of her Welsh chapel, to which she felt she belonged wherever she might be, attendance at Sunday School never seemed to draw out the best in her. She could be quite a defiant little girl, and on one occasion drew the surprised eyes of the teachers on her when she suddenly started to sing a music hall ditty she had certainly not learned from them.

'Daisy, Daisy, give me your answer do!
I'm half crazy, all for the love of you . . .'

The little voice was singing very clearly, dancing steadily over the remonstrating 'shush's' that tried in vain to stay its course. 'Quiet, darling!' was a fence which merely served as an incentive to a high-spirited increase in volume, and she sang on :

'It won't be a stylish marriage,
We can't afford a carriage . . .'

A gentle but firm adult arm whisking her off her feet warned her she would not be allowed to stay, and even at that early age Margaret sensed that resistance would be futile. But whatever happened, she was going to finish her song. As the diminutive, be-ribboned little girl with the large light blue eyes was carried out of the chapel, the last line of the ditty came out with a rush, and everyone heard it :

'But-you'll-look-sweet-upon-the-seat-of-a-bicycle-
made-for-two!'

Underneath the quiet, gentle exterior there was a determination of character that all who knew her well recognised, and it was evident at a very early age.

When she was three years old her mother died and her father, unable to look after her himself, reluctantly parted with her and she went to live with her grandmother. Four years were to pass before the father re-married, and Margaret returned to a normal family life. Those disturbed earlier years seemed to pass from her memory so completely that when Mrs Morgan, with an instinctive reticence about usurping another's place, sometimes referred to herself as being merely Margaret's stepmother, Margaret eventually said to her,

'Please don't say that, Mum. I don't feel a bit like that about you. I don't remember my own mother—you're the only mother I've ever known. *You're* my Mum!' And she meant it. Years later, when she was a missionary in Thailand, her colleagues there all knew that home to Margaret was the little terrace house in Porth where Mum lived, and where her friends were always sure of a welcome.

She had pronounced likes and dislikes when it came to food.

'Would I have to eat parsnips?' was her immediate reaction as a child to a suggestion made one day by Aunt Flo:

'Margaret, what if the Lord should call you to be a missionary?' Aunt Flo herself was a member of the China Inland Mission, and spent long holidays in the Morgan home in Porth when on furlough. Her talks about life in the Far East were inspiring to those ready to respond to the challenge of sacrifice and high endeavour, but to her little great-niece the deepest impression made at the time was a fear of unappetising food, epitomised for her in the detested parsnip.

Aunt Flo was a great reader of books and maker of notes on them, too, spending hours with her Bible propped up in front of her, presumably preparing lessons for her Bible School students in far-away China. This sort of life made no appeal to Margaret, who for all her quiet manner was high-spirited enough when it came to walking along high walls to the alarm of passers-by and somersaulting over any available railings when waiting at a bus stop. Bert Taylor saw her sometimes, coat flying and flapping around her as she ran out from the Ferndale Secondary School, and delightedly she would respond to his invitation of a lift home on the back of his motor-bike. Her favourite lessons at school were games and physical training, and her ambition was to become a ballet dancer. This idea, as might have been expected, was firmly squashed at home, and there were times when a sulky silence enveloped the small schoolgirl in her gym tunic sitting at the table in the living room, unwillingly doing her homework. Why couldn't she be allowed to go to dancing classes? Why must she sit and write in exercise books at home, when she'd been doing that at school all day? But the sulks never lasted long, and she was soon singing again —once her homework was done.

'Margaret could do much better if she tried', was a remark that frequently appeared on her school reports, but when the suggestion was made that she might study better if she went into the front room where she could be alone and away from the music of the radio, she refused to go. She didn't want to be alone, she didn't want to be quiet, and she liked working to the sound of music.

'Afraid of missing something!' her father remarked sagely, and probably he was right. She liked to know what was going on, and what went on at home went on in the living room at the back. It would have been far too disturbing to be isolated in the narrow front room, trying to concentrate on sums and grammar and geography when there was the lively hum of conversation and the clatter of cups with visitors always coming to the home tantalisingly separated from her by a thick wall. It was much easier to concentrate on her lessons when there were people around. There was nothing of the recluse about her, and even in her later years, when the mystical side of her nature developed to an unusual degree, she never lost her intense interest in people.

She wasn't a shy child, either, although for the first twelve years of her life she was an only child. She thoroughly enjoyed taking part in Sunday School anniversaries when she had the opportunity of performing, and willingly recited the texts she had learned at the front of the chapel on Sunday mornings. And on week-nights, as soon as her books could be stuffed into her satchel, she would be off to dress up and play at acting with her friends, one of whom had a cellar under her home which saw the production of many a drama.

Dolls played no part in her life at all. She sang and she swam, she struggled with needle and thread until she had learned to sew, but the friends and relatives who from time to time presented her with a doll were disappointed if they had expected to see her playing with it. She looked at it with an expression as devoid of feeling as the doll's own, and quietly put it aside. She was not interested.

It was a different matter when Mum had a baby, giving Dad another daughter, and Margaret a sister! Margaret was twelve years old by this time, and the excitement and pleasure of seeing a real live little bundle of humanity sleeping peacefully in its cot or kicking in its bath, brought something to life within her that no-one had realised was there. 'She's a born nurse!' Dad exclaimed, watching her pick up the screaming baby and pacify her, deftly unpin a soiled nappy and replace it with a clean one, hold her comfortably so that she sucked milk contentedly from her bottle. 'I don't know how I'd manage without you,' he told her in the difficult months that followed, when Mum was laid up with a severe spinal injury that took her into hospital for several weeks. His schoolgirl daughter was behaving with an evident sense of responsibility he had not known she possessed, and he was proud of her.

In that twelfth year of her life something else happened of even greater significance. A well-known evangelist came to Porth for a series of meetings, and during the course of that evangelistic campaign Margaret, along with four other

girls in the same Sunday School, came to personal faith in
the Lord Jesus Christ. What had been heard from early childhood and accepted with the same impersonal belief as his-
torical facts like the coming to England of William the Con-
queror in 1066, suddenly became alive and real and intimate.
Jesus Christ, who was born in a manger in Bethlehem nearly
two thousand years ago, and who had died nailed to a cross
outside the walls of Jerusalem at the age of thirty-three, was
the Son of God himself. He was alive today. He had risen
from the dead and ascended into heaven, and that meant He
was there now. He knew all about her, Margaret Morgan,
and was ready and willing to impart to her a new life, a
principle within which would enable her to become the sort
of woman God meant her to be. She did not know at all what
it would involve, but in that little stone chapel she knelt one
evening and accepted what God was offering her—and
asked Him to accept her, for life and for eternity.

There was nothing spectacular about it. There was perhaps little outward difference in the schoolgirl who had,
after all, been connected with the chapel from early childhood, and whose continued attendance at the meetings was
no more than would be expected in view of the sort of home
she came from. She still found study irksome, and made it
quite plain that she did not intend staying on at school a day
longer than the law demanded. No amount of persuasion at
home could prevail on her to alter her mind about this, and
she refused to stay on to take her 'O' levels. Obtaining a
job as typist in the same firm in which her father was em-
ployed she developed a taste for expensive clothes, like many
other girls in the adolescent stage, and viewed with a critical
eye the lino on the floors at home, which compared un-
favourably with the carpets on the floors of some of the
people she knew. She was often absent-minded, and was
liable to mislay her keys. Altogether, as a young teenager,
Margaret differed little from many other girls with a similar
background and mentality.

Except in one respect.

This was her propensity for cultivating spiritual friendships, which later became one of her distinguishing characteristics. She loved the company of those with whom she could speak freely of inward spiritual experiences, with whom she could pray and sing in conscious harmony. The enrichment of her life with God meant more to her than the excitements of outings with contemporaries and the attentions of boy friends. Gradually she withdrew from the circles of former companions, spending more and more of her free time in the home of Bert and Alma Taylor.

This hospitable couple, who had two boys of their own, encouraged young people to come to tea on Saturdays and Sundays, and conversation usually led eventually to discussions about the Christian way of life, to the study of the Bible, and to the hymn-singing that springs so naturally from Welsh throats. To be a Christian was a joyous experience, but it was a solemn one, too, requiring not only faith but patience, humility, steadfastness and love, qualities which do not blossom automatically any more than do luscious grapes without a pruning knife. When the Man of Galilee offered eternal life to His followers He did not attempt to disguise the fact that it would be accompanied by suffering, that it would demand renunciations, even to the laying down of life itself, in a mystical if not in a practical sense. Bert and Alma made this plain, but with a sincerity which attracted many young people, Margaret among them. The friendship formed then lasted all her life, and she became one of the most regular visitors to their home.

It was through her association with another married couple, again some years older than herself, that Margaret was started on the path that eventually led her to Thailand. These friends had moved from Porth to Bath, and knowing Margaret had nowhere to go for her holiday one year, invited her to spend it with them. Margaret found herself in a hospitable home where there was much coming and going of young people, among them some nurses from nearby hospitals who were glad to take advantage of an open invitation to visit on their free days. No-one knew just what or who had influenced her, how or when it happened, but at the end of her fortnight's holiday she announced that she wanted to apply to the Bristol Royal Infirmary to be enrolled as a student nurse. Her friends were surprised. 'Well, that's fine—if it's the Lord's will,' they said cautiously. 'But make sure it's not a passing impression.' At home family and friends, employer and fellow employees were all convinced it was emotion and all reacted against the idea with differing degrees of intensity. A nursing career was excellent for girls who were physically and nervously robust, but Margaret was obviously not strong enough for it. She'd never stick the long hours and the heavy lifting, the running around and the study.

'You tire too quickly.'

'The hours are too irregular. You'll lose out on sleep.'

'Your health just won't stand it. And you'll never be able to lift heavy patients. You haven't the physical strength for it.'

'You know how easily you get headaches. Colds, too. You pick up a cold so quickly when you're run down . . .'

But Margaret was adamant, and she gave as her reason the conviction that God meant her to become a nurse and a missionary. She was sure that this was the path she should take, and even the reminder that she had no 'O' levels to her credit, and without them could scarcely expect to be accepted into training, did not deter her. A new way of life had opened up before her during that fortnight's holiday, and she must go forward into whatever it was the Lord had prepared for her. She would have no peace of mind if she hung back. Eventually her parents gave a reluctant permission for her to go ahead, and she made her application.

It was humiliating to have to admit she had no 'O' levels, and she regretted her obstinacy in refusing to stay on at school and sit for them when she had the opportunity. However, the matron told her that if she could pass the Intelligence Test she could be accepted. It took her three hours to answer the questions set, but she came through the ordeal successfully, and in September 1952 she entered the Preliminary Training School of the Bristol Royal Infirmary.

'She'll be back before the month is up!' was a prophecy that proved to be wrong. Margaret's experiences in the three years that followed were little different from those of most girls doing their nursing training. If she was more exhausted than the average nurse when coming off duty and needed longer to sleep off her weariness than the others in her set, she managed to struggle out of bed and into her uniform in time for lectures or reporting on the wards. She loved the practical side of the work, and those comments on her school reports 'Margaret could do much better if she tried' proved true as she got down to the necessary study. She did not escape the trials, common to nurses in training, of working under nursing sisters whose temperaments created tensions, and there were occasions when her monthly visits home were clouded by apprehension as to whom she would have to work under when she returned to hospital. But she made lasting friends during those years at Bristol, among the Nurses Christian Union particularly. One of them was the robust, bright-eyed sister in the Casualty Department. Her name was Brenda Holton, she came from Liverpool, and she was preparing to be a missionary somewhere in southeast Asia.

Neither of them had any idea in those days when they worked together in Casualty, and met to share responsibility for the weekly meetings of the Christian Union, that Brenda was destined to lead the way into the rural leprosy clinics in South Thailand.

CHAPTER TWO

BEARER OF BURDENS

From Margaret Morgan's notebook

Why, Lord, the heartache
the emptiness, the darkness
and the loneliness?
Why the disappointment
with others, with circumstances,
and most of all with myself?

Why is it, Lord,
that I don't see Your face
hear Your voice
feel Your love?

My child, you do not know now
but one day you will.
Trust Me, even though you cannot
see My face
hear My voice
feel My love.
Because your senses are dimmed
It does not mean that I am far away
that I don't care
that I am withholding My love.

I would have you remember that
Through suffering
He was made perfect
By the things that He suffered
He learnt obedience.
As I dealt with My Son
so I deal with you.
As He trusted Me
so you must trust Me.
Remember My child,
You walk by faith
not by sight,
With your eyes on Me
and not on yourself,
or others
or circumstances.

Through this time trust Me child,
Trust Me to refine
to strengthen, to perfect,
Trust Me to make you
like My Son,
My Beloved, in Whom I delight.
                              M.M.

THE DIFFERENCES IN the early experiences of Margaret and Minka were as pronounced as in their appearance. Margaret was petite and easily lost sight of in a crowd. Minka was six feet tall, and a striking figure in any company. Margaret's life until she went to Thailand was uneventful and her course unimpeded by any major calamities. Minka's, on the other hand, was tumultuous and varied, beset with change and obstacles, though enriched by a passionate family loyalty and devotion to God which supported her in the midst of the horrors of a Japanese internment camp.

Even her birth was attended by surprise and excitement, for she was born just before midnight on Queen Wilhelmina's birthday in 1922, when the nationwide revelry in honour of Holland's popular monarch was only just subsiding. Young Mr and Mrs Hanskamp had, in fact, arranged to entertain a party of friends in their first-floor flat in the square in Maassluis on that very occasion, but had to cancel it in a hurry when it became evident that their first child would be arriving ahead of schedule.

Minka's smile, which characterised her throughout her life, came into play at a very early age. Her father, who was a school teacher, was asked by the distracted parents of an apparently uncontrollable boy if he could undertake to discipline the lad. Mr Hanskamp set about it in a kindly way, and among other things sent the boy out marketing for his wife. On his return he was allowed, as a reward, to go and

look at the baby in the cradle. He would go and stand looking down at Minka, and when she opened her eyes and
gurgled and smiled, he would call out delightedly, 'She
smiled at me! She smiled at me!' Teacher Hanskamp and
his wife attributed their success in turning a naughty boy
into a good one to prayer, and to Minka's smile.

A few months after Minka was born her father, returning
with his wife from church one Sunday said, 'My dear, I think
the time has come for us to go to Indonesia.' For some years
the thought of serving God in that country had been in his
mind, and now an invitation had reached him through the
Dutch Reformed Church to go to Java as principal of a
school for Chinese children. Very significantly a verse from
Isaiah's prophecy had confirmed that the waiting time was
over. 'For you shall not go out in haste, and you shall not go
in flight, for the Lord will go before you, and the God of
Israel will be your rearguard.' So when Minka was a year
old she was taken from the flat, low-lying country of her
birth to the mountainous land of Java with its rich tropical
foliage and its colourful people. Here her sisters and
brothers were born, here she herself became like a child of
Java, running barefoot around the large school and hospital
compounds of the Mission, in and out of Indonesian and
Chinese homes.

It was in one of these that she one day saw something happen which sent her speeding back to her mother in great
excitement.

'Oh, Mama!' she cried. 'I've seen such a wonderful thing.
It was in one of the Chinese houses, and a baby was born. I
saw it all. I saw how the baby was born, and what the nurse
did, and oh, it was marvellous! And I saw it!'

Mrs Hanskamp, with her European upbringing, was pro-
foundly disturbed that her little daughter, not yet ten, should
have been brought so close to the intimacies of human life.
'That little daughter of yours has the hands of a midwife,'
the Mission doctor had told her once, but she had not
wanted her to be introduced to the profession so early. For

Minka, however, the experience contained no horror. She had had a glimpse into one of the mysteries of creation, that life is born out of suffering, and that the joy of that life swallows up all the sorrow preceding it. And she had seen the skill of firm yet gentle hands at work with insistent pressure, aiding the process of birth and also easing the pain. Was the desire born in her then that one day her own hands would do that?

Minka, for all her vitality, was a quiet child with a depth of feeling for the weakness of others which made her very early in life the nurse and guardian of younger children. She entertained the doctor's children as well as her own brothers and sisters for hours, singing with them and producing little plays for them to act. Somehow she herself was always in the background. Her two animated, attractive little sisters were likely to be in the leading roles, both off the stage and on. But Mrs Hanskamp knew that whatever happened, Minka would be there—especially when things went wrong.

Ann and Alice were arguing, and Minka was trying to pacify them.

Gerald had wandered away alone, and Minka was looking for him.

John had fallen over, and Minka was bringing him in to have his cuts washed.

Baby Margaret had stopped screaming because Minka had picked her up.

She was too busy looking after the others to get into much mischief herself, and from the parents' point of view she was a good child. But Minka herself knew otherwise. One afternoon during the siesta her mother found her in bed with a Bible picture book on her knees, crying bitterly. The reason she gave for her tears, when asked, was that it was so awful to think of all the Lord Jesus had suffered on the cross just because *she*, Minka, was so often naughty and didn't do what she was told.

In 1935, the year after Margaret Morgan was born in

South Wales, Minka Hanskamp went back to Holland to complete her education there, living in the town of Arnhem with relatives. Everything was changed for her now. Brilliant blue tropical skies gave place to cloudy ones through which the sun shone but dimly. Instead of the colour and variety of the large compounds with their lush tropical foliage where she could run barefooted, were well-ordered households, and quiet streets devoid of food stalls and vendors, along which one walked sedately, always neatly clothed and shod. Worst of all, she was alone, separated from the family that was the centre of her life and affection. They were not happy years for her, and the outbreak of war in Europe, which brought suffering to so many millions, proved to be her reason for escape. It was decided that with the Nazi armies on the march on land and Nazi warships proving their superiority at sea, Minka must be sent back to her parents in Indonesia. The sinking of a Dutch ship in November brought home the urgency of the matter, and December 1939 saw Minka joyfully embarking for the journey home to rejoin her family in the city of Bandung for two of the happiest and most normal years of her life. They saw the completion of her education in the Bandung High School, the birth of her youngest brother Peter, the beginning of a friendship that might have ripened to love and marriage, and her personal commitment to Jesus Christ.

Then came 7th December, 1941. With simultaneous air attacks on Pearl Harbor, Manila and Hawaii Japan declared war on the Allies. Before the end of the month Japanese forces had landed in Malaya, the Philippines and Sarawak, while Hong Kong had surrendered. By the end of January New Guinea and the Solomon Islands had been invaded, and in February came the numbing news that after a week's fighting Singapore had surrendered.

The following day the Japanese landed in Sumatra. The invasion of Indonesia had begun.

Minka by this time was working as a secretary in the headquarters of General Wavell's forces in Bandung. She had given her oath that she would not divulge anything she heard there, and as news came over the secret radio from military and government sources of the progress of the war, she heard things intended only for those in high command, and was warned of the vital necessity of passing on her information to no-one. She returned home day after day, silent and white-faced, her lips pursed together. She knew something that her father, intently as he listened to the general news over the radio, did not know. The invasion of Java was imminent.

'Father, I think it would be a good idea for you to put food in the air raid shelters,' was all she said one day when she knew that air raids would soon become fierce.

But it was not long before everyone knew that Java had surrendered, and it was only a matter of time before enemy soldiers would enter the city. And the hush of fear descended.

'It's the Korean soldiers who come first,' it was whispered. 'They're ruthless . . . stop at nothing. And they'll want women . . .'

'The girls . . .! We must hide the girls . . .!'

The defenders of the city had gone by this time, and everyone who could flee had fled, the boy who was Minka's friend among them. There was nothing anyone could do to save others now, and young men were those in the greatest danger. They might be shot at sight! Let them get away as best they may, get to the coast, find a ship, any sort of ship going anywhere—anywhere away from the enemy. But the girls can't go like that. They mustn't be seen. We must hide the girls . . .

So Minka and Ann and Alice were secreted in a little room with a big cupboard pushed in front of the door to hide it, and there they remained for weeks, until the tall fierce soldiers conscripted from Korea had gone, and the Japanese civil authorities had taken over.

Things weren't too bad at first, although of course there were restrictions. Everyone must register. All radios were confiscated. No travelling without a permit. Dutch refugees arrived from mid-Java, and some were housed with the Hanskamps. Thirty years later, recalling those early days, Mrs Hanskamp said :

'Of course it was a very difficult time for us all. But I remember that we often laughed. We could see the funny side of things, and when something amusing happened, or someone told a joke, we would laugh heartily.'

It was not so easy to laugh when Mr Hanskamp was arrested, along with a number of other men holding Dutch passports, and taken off to an internment camp. It was possible to visit him at first and take little food parcels, but soon he was moved away and they did not know where he had been taken. Then a portion of Bandung city was cordoned off behind high bamboo walls and barbed wire, and some twelve thousand Dutch women and children were herded into it. The Hanskamp family were thankful to be together, though in a very small house, until the proclamation went forth that the boys were to be taken to other camps. Gerald, aged fifteen, was marched away first. Then, some time later, as the age groups were getting lower and lower, John had to go, too. He was ten years old.

Food was getting scarcer. The daily rations were decreasing, and if you didn't guard what you had someone would steal it. It was amazing the people who would slyly make off with someone else's sugar or bread or rice. Food. It was becoming the main subject for thought and conversation. Some of the old women would sit in little groups, planning menus, discussing the meals they would like to make. Some of the younger women, succumbing to hunger, found a way of obtaining what they wanted. After all, the guards were men ...

All the time things were getting worse. They were moved to another camp, even more congested. Then came the transfer by train to an unknown destination. Each person was allowed to take twenty kilos of belongings, no more, and anyone too weak to carry her twenty kilos must do without them. 'Hurry up, get on the train, quick, quick!' So into the train they struggled, crushed together in the semi-darkness, for the windows were all shuttered, and for two days and two nights rumbled on, without food, without water. Tuberculosis was rife in the camp by this time, and many people died on that train. When eventually they arrived at Djakarta, the only place for the Hanskamps to live was in the little room that had been the morgue. After a time they were moved again, to Tjideng, the worst camp of all.

Every day you lined up for the roll call, and every night, too. If you didn't bow to the Japanese officer you were beaten. On the other hand, if you bowed too low, you were also beaten, as to bow too low was to insult him. If the Camp Commandant was angry about something it might mean punishment drill for the whole camp, standing for hours in the sun as it beat down mercilessly on your head, the ground beneath you hot like an oven. If you saw your neighbour swaying and knew she was going to faint, you knew you must not help her. If she fell down the guard would come and kick her till she got up again—or until he saw she could not move, when he'd just leave her there. You knew that if you fell over it would be the same for you so you held on to your strength through the interminable hours, a cry to God in your heart. You had to hold on to God in those days, meet together in little groups to pray and read the Bible, however weary you were. You knew it was life and sanity to you to do it. You saw others going insane, becoming thieves for a morsel of bread, losing grip on themselves so that their despair led to demoralisation. But if you kept those invisible channels of prayer open, by faith asking for and receiving the Divine Life, you knew you could endure; endure the filth and the stench and the flies, and the hunger and the weariness and the pain, because through it all Christ was with you, and there were those golden moments when His very Presence seemed to bathe you in peace ...

So those long dark years passed, with Minka threading her way through them, nursing in the camp hospital, shouldering responsibility for the family so that, looking back, Alice said, 'It really didn't seem so very bad at the time. I think it was because Minka was there. Somehow she took the burden, shielded us. She was the eldest and we looked to her, relied on her.'

Yes, Minka was there. When permission was obtained in the early days in the Bandung camp to go out and buy food occasionally, it was Minka who set off on an old tricycle, returning from the Chinese shop at the bottom of the hill panting but triumphant with her stores. Later on, when Mama was ill and restrictions were tightened, it was Minka whose urgent prayers brought a miraculous response as, walking round the perimeter of the camp she heard the name 'Hanskamp!' whispered, and a basket of food was thrust through the barbed wire into her outstretched arms. Indonesian and Chinese friends sent parcels of food from time to time, through the Red Cross, but she never knew from whom that mysterious bundle came, with its provisions that were just what her mother needed.

She knew how provision of another sort was procured later on, in the last, terrible camp at Tjideng, though. She had noticed that her mother was beginning to swell, and with the medical knowledge she obtained from the Dutch doctors in the hospital, she knew the cause. Her mother needed more protein. And there was no more protein. But she learned that there is protein in snails, so Minka went round the camp quietly collecting snails. Then she made a concoction of them, sprinkled it with pepper, and giving it to her mother said,

'Mama, don't ask what this is. Just eat it.'

There were times, of course, when there was no provision at all. The day after Mrs Hanskamp's birthday, when her daughters had secretly parted with their bread ration to procure a cup as a present for her, it was announced that there would be no rations for anyone for three days. 'Don't

worry, Mama,' they said, seeing her distress. She felt as
David felt when the three mighty men, at the risk of their
lives, brought him water from the well at Bethlehem. 'We
are so glad we were able to get the cup for your birthday. It's
what we wanted to do, and it made us happy to do it.'

Food or no food, however, they had to go on working.
Weak as they were they were glad to get out into the fields
to carry stones, or dig, or plant. It was better to be out in the
open, in spite of the blazing sun, than to be cooped up in
the camp with its noisome odour of death. But when the
girls were detailed to do furniture removing, loading pianos,
refrigerators, stoves on to lorries, it seemed too much. 'We
can't. We haven't got the strength. We *can't* lift those
things . . .'

But when they knew that the mothers and children in the
camp were being kept standing out in the broiling sun until
the task was completed, somehow they did it.

Minka herself became very ill in that Tjideng camp, so
ill that the doctors said to each other as they stood looking
at her, 'She won't be long—she'll be dead in a few hours.'
They did not know she could hear them, nor that something
within her said defiantly, 'No, I won't!' The life within her
nearly flickered out, but not quite, and slowly she recovered.

Perhaps the darkest hour for Minka was one night when
she had stolen back to the camp hospital, which was against
Japanese orders, to see one of the patients she had been
nursing during the day. She knew how se/erely she would
be punished if she were caught. The two beatings she had
already received for minor offences would be mild compared with what she would have to suffer in the camp gaol.
But her concern for some of her patients was so intense
that she often made the journey back to see them after
nightfall. 'Oh, God, send your angels to hide me,' she
prayed earnestly before she set out, and always she returned
eventually, unnoticed. 'I always feel safe when Minka is
about,' one of the Dutch doctors told her mother, 'She
seems to have special protection.'

On this occasion she returned again, safely, but when she got to the strip of floor that was hers in the crowded room, she flung herself down and burst into tears.

'Oh, why?' she sobbed. 'Why all this suffering? What does God want with it all? Why does He allow it?'

Why? To what purpose this desolation, this apparent triumph of evil and death? Why must man in his weakness and extremity be forsaken? She had been kneeling beside a dying woman whom she knew and loved, and the sight of the suffering she could not alleviate, the accumulated sense of the misery of the camp had plumbed depths of feeling that cried out at last for an answer, a reason for it all. Why? It was a cry from her heart too profound to be quietened by human sympathy or explanations, and at last she sobbed herself to sleep. She rose as usual the next morning, and went about the arduous routine of the camp without any outward change. But the question remained in her heart for a long long time. Only the Man of Calvary, whose own cry, 'My God, my God, why hast Thou forsaken me?' revealed an even deeper agony, could give her the answer of love that eventually silenced the question.

No news from the outside world reached the camp, of course, and the end of the war that came so suddenly in August, 1945, with the unconditional surrender of Japan nine days after the explosion of the first atomic bomb on Hiroshima, brought relief but slowly to the internees in Indonesia. Only the changed attitude of the Japanese guards, the relaxing of restrictions and the cessation of punishments gave hope that the war was over. Even when a truck load of white men drove triumphantly into the camp one day, bringing assurance of victory and better food supplies, living conditions could not be greatly improved. Indonesia, liberated from Japanese domination, was strongly resistant to any suggestion that it should return to the old Dutch colonial system, and was demanding its independence. Groups of young men were already taking militant action, and Dutch women and children were likely to be safer now inside the camps than outside, until the toll of those who had died in internment had been taken, those who remained re-united with their families and arrangements made for their repatriation to Holland. Day after day the women crowded round the lists that appeared at the entrance of the camps, scanning the names of the men there to see if those they loved were on the live list—or the list of those who had died.

The arrival of Mr Hanskamp, unheralded, was met with unbelief at first when a little girl came with the news, 'Your daddy is at the front of the camp. He says come and see him!'

'Don't joke about things like that!' said Mrs Hanskamp sharply. It was too serious a matter to be made the subject for fun. The tension of waiting for news made one too taut, too fearful . . .

'All right then! Don't believe me!' said the child, offended, and walked off. There was something about her attitude that prompted Alice to say,

'Mama, why don't you go and look? I suppose it's just possible he's come.' And sure enough, he was there, thin, scarcely recognisable with his drawn face, but Father himself, smiling at them. He had lived through even worse things than they, but he had lived through, and here he was at last. Gerald too. And John. The Hanskamp family had all survived the long ordeal, and in 1946 they returned to Holland.

The next ten years for Minka held a series of disappointments and setbacks, which commenced shortly after she arrived in Holland. With the training and experience in nursing she had received in the internment camp it was expected she would be considered eligible to sit immediately for the final nursing examinations and start work as a fully-qualified nurse. To her dismay she learned that the lectures arranged under such difficulties, and delivered with such meticulous care by the Dutch camp doctors and nurses in Indonesia went for nothing. The constant battle with death, the experience gained in nursing under-nourished, dispirited internees back to health, the ingenuity exercised in producing appetising meals when rations were so low that grains of rice were sometimes counted out one by one — it was all irrelevant now, when new techniques were being introduced, and new drugs of which she had never even heard were being prescribed. At the age of twenty-four, therefore, she entered a hospital in Amsterdam to commence her official training.

Two months later she heard that her mother was seriously ill. Impulsively she hurried back home to look after her, indifferent to the protests of the matron, and thereby forfeited her position in the training school. There followed a period of uncertainty as the door to midwifery training opened, closed, and opened again. Eventually, in the autumn of 1947, she re-entered training and four years later, as a qualified nurse and midwife, began enquiring of missionary societies in Holland about the possibility of service overseas.

She was not encouraged. There were national midwives on the mission field now, and there was no openings for her in that capacity. The answer was always the same. The missionary societies did not want missionary nurses.

By this time the family was scattering, and her sister Alice had married and gone to settle in New Zealand. It was from this country that she wrote to Minka, explaining that many of the wives of immigrants there did not like going to hospital to have their babies, but preferred a private midwife. Why not come to New Zealand? It might be that here the Lord had a special work for her to do. So Minka, over thirty by this time, went to New Zealand and started learning another language. If she were to live and work in New Zealand, she must learn English. After eighteen months' diligent, steady study she spoke with scarcely a trace of a Dutch accent, and wrote so well that only the occasional quaint turn of phrase betrayed that she had not been born and brought up in an English-speaking community. She obtained her SRN and SCM without difficulty.

There were plenty of opportunities for her exceptional nursing skills in New Zealand, and once people knew her there was a welcome everywhere for the tall young woman from Holland, with her wide smile and readiness to laugh at herself. She made friends quickly, though she was not an easy conversationalist, preferring to stand back and let others do the talking. Alice's home, always open to her, was a place where she loved to be, for the family of nephews and nieces responded to her ardent affection, and she was always happiest when she could be among children. Altogether, there was no evident reason why she should not settle down to life in New Zealand with great satisfaction, and for a time she did so, moving frequently and earning a good deal of money. Then she became restless. She was not satisfied and could not understand why.

How could she know that a little group of missionaries who had withdrawn from China under Communist pressure in 1951 had gone to the south of Thailand with the object of proclaiming the Gospel of Christ to the Muslim population there? How could she know that as they wrestled with the new languages, Thai and Malay, that must be learned, as they tried to adapt from the cold, crisp climate of north China to the humid, enervating heat of the tropics, it was borne in on them increasingly that other, younger people must complete the task they could only hope to begin? Who was to tell her that those missionaries, as they knelt together for their daily periods of worship, were acting on the instructions their Master had laid down, to pray to the Lord of the harvest that He would thrust forth labourers into His harvest?

No-one told her in so many words. She had heard of the China Inland Mission when in Java as a child, but knew nothing about its several hundred workers who had left China to start their missionary lives all over again in the countries of south-east Asia. All she knew was that, as she expressed it herself:

'In September, 1955, I understood that the work I was doing did not satisfy me. After much praying the Lord said, "I want to use you." I did not know how. I was travelling a lot at the time and couldn't talk the matter over with someone.' In the following April she made an approach to a missionary organisation, but received no reply, and then,

'I became very homesick, and booked to go home. After that peace was gone. I attended some of Dr Orr's team meetings. At the last meeting I felt urged to put my hand up. I was taken to one of the little rooms and then promised the Lord I would not go home, but go out for Him. Peace came back.

'I had no idea what to do next. Then my mother wrote to me about the CIM. I went to the Crusaders' bookroom and asked the gentleman whether he knew the address of CIM.'

She was getting on the track at last, for the man in the bookroom had been in the CIM himself. He knew not only the address, but the Home Director's telephone number, and put through a call then and there, making an appointment for Minka to see him the following evening. Except in one respect she felt the interview was satisfactory. This Mission which depended so deliberately on God for the supply of its material needs, and was working in southeast Asia, the very area to which she felt drawn, would be one in which she would be happy. Furthermore, no suggestion was made that there would be no opening for one with her qualifications as nurse and midwife to work there. There was only one drawback, and that was a major one, which she could not rectify.

'My age was the problem. I left rather disappointed.'

She returned to Alice Van Zweeden's home that evening unusually depressed. She was over thirty now, and another two years must be added before she could apply to the CIM, for she must first have Bible College training. There was the Bible College in Auckland of which she had heard, but even if she were accepted as a student (and who could tell whether she wouldn't be too old for that, too?) she had no assurance from the CIM that she would be eligible to join its ranks. It scarcely seemed worth the trouble to get in touch with the College. Better give up the idea of missionary work, and settle into nursing in New Zealand . . .

But—when Abraham was called out of Ur, he went though he did not know where he was going. When the Children of Israel were faced with the impassable Red Sea, they were told to go forward, and they went forward. When Philip the evangelist was told to leave his fruitful ministry in Samaria and go to the desert, he went. The insistent pressure within Minka urged her to take the one step that was possible. There was nothing to prevent her writing to the Principal of the Bible College.

'I remained restless until I wrote for the application form.' And now she had filled it in. 'I have done what I could. I leave the rest entirely to Him.' She read over her answers to the questions again, and felt they were not likely to make a very good impression. But she must be truthful. 'I have backslidden during the last two years of war. After two years I was restored to fellowship.' It did not occur to her to offer excuse or explanation. From her point of view, there were the bare facts, and the record of her Christian life would not be complete without them. 'My friend became a real Christian after we had been talking and praying for months,' she had written in answer to the question whether she had ever led anyone to Christ, but it would be presenting an unbalanced picture without adding the words, 'But she already knew about Christ because her parents belonged to church.' She had had conversations about the Saviour with patients, 'but I don't know if these talks have led to something.'

She signed the papers and posted them off. She had taken the one step that was open to her, and now she must await the result. It led to the next step. Almost to her surprise she was accepted as a student of the Bible College, and at the age of thirty-four started yet another sort of training. Now the way ahead was to become increasingly clear. Although she was one of the oldest of the students, and came from a church background different from the others, the Principal of the College observed that there were 'no personality problems with this woman'. As a team worker she was 'loved by all', and she had 'a sweet disposition, attractive personality; not aggressive, but with gifts which command confidence and a following'. So when Mr J. O. Sanders, General Director of the CIM Overseas Missionary Fellowship, visited the Bible College some months after Minka had entered it as a student, and was told that the tall, grey-haired student over there pouring out tea was Minka Hanskamp, he strolled over to her and said pleasantly:

'I hear you're interested in the Overseas Missionary Fellowship? I think you'd be wise to apply straight away . . .'

So the usual processes were set in motion, with interviews, and questionnaires sent out to referees, and a report from the Principal of the Bible College. This report was favourable from beginning to end, and concluded with a simple sentence which would have amazed Minka, always with an excessively low opinion of herself, had she read it.

'We would recommend Minka without reserve to represent Christ anywhere in the world.'

CHAPTER THREE

BEGINNING AGAIN

From Margaret Morgan's notebook

My child, I need to teach you patience
My work is not done in a day.
I work quietly, slowly
Yet persistently.
You must believe that I am working
even though you see little evidence
and you are tempted
to doubt and discouragement.
When you have asked something of Me, My child,
Something consistent with My character
Something you know I would give,
would do,

Trust Me to give, trust Me to act
in My own way
and in My own time.
You know, My child,
I am Your Father
A Father all-loving
One who gives abundantly
out of a heart
full of compassion and love.
One who knows the need of your
spirit, body and soul.
Be patient and trust Me to work,
Know that I am a God
'Who works for those who wait for Him.'
                                        M.M.

When a field problem in South Thailand was much on her heart, and she was tempted to offer advice.

ABOUT THE TIME when Minka was applying unsuccessfully to missionary societies in Holland, and Margaret was starting nursing training in Bristol, four missionaries were settling in to a corner house on a street in Yala, a Thai town near the border of Malaya. They had left China along with hundreds of others in 1951, and been designated to pioneer missionary work among the Malays, who were Muslims, living in the four southern provinces of Thailand. It would not have been surprising if, as they sank wearily underneath their mosquito nets at the end of the day, with shouts from the nearby boxing ring effectively holding sleep at bay, they sometimes wondered if they would make the grade in this assignment. The youngest of them was entering the somewhat indeterminate period of life designated as middle-age, while the eldest might be said to be emerging from it. Yet here they were, in a very hot country with an enervating climate, living cheek by jowl with people whose language they did not understand, and starting their missionary life all over again.

The only people with whom they could communicate with any degree of success were the Chinese merchants they met in the market. Their hesitant and limited Thai, laboriously learned in a crash course in Bangkok, did not get them much farther than a superficial talk about visas and passports with polite and charming local officials. The Malays themselves, said to comprise eighty per cent of the population, all seemed to live out of town, mysteriously melting away, after marketing or visiting the mosque, into the jungles and plantations that surrounded Yala, elusive as the Muslims of north-west China.

'We're going to have a job to get in touch with them at all,' the missionaries agreed, fanning themselves vigorously after a visit to their neighbours to distribute tracts. 'Let alone learn their language!' In one respect at least there was a similarity between the place they had come from and the place in which they now found themselves. The Muslims were equally difficult to reach in either. Their women might be freer, moving about the streets in colourful sarongs, apparently unrestricted by the customs that had held their dark-robed sisters in the north-west of China confined to walled compounds. Their vendors of fruit and dried fish, rice and squawking fowls might flood the markets and crowd the buses till the town seemed full of them, but when it came to house-to-house visiting in the streets of Yala the missionaries found Chinese and Thai, Pakistanis and Indians living there, but rarely any Malays. The mosques and Islamic schools for boys were plentiful, it is true, but as three of the missionary team were women there was little they could do about visiting those exclusively male institutions. In any case, a knowledge of the Malay language was essential, and as the majority of the Malays were illiterate, and as no language course for foreigners was available locally, how would they set about learning it? They eventually found a Malay pundit willing to teach them, but to obtain the social contacts necessary to practise conversation was difficult.

With the Thai it was different. They lived next door, and on the same street, and with gentle courtesy welcomed the westerners who had come to live in their country. With the Chinese and the Indians and the Pakistanis thinly scattered in the community it was also different. Some of them spoke a little English. All of them, like the missionaries, needed to speak Thai, the language of the country, and there were other points of contact making for friendly relationships. There were even a few, a very few, Christians among them, and it was with these that the first simple Sunday services were held in the missionaries' home. But how to get alongside the Malays, outwardly so friendly yet in reality so aloof, clinging tenaciously to their own language, their own culture, above all their own religion? They might be very conscious of being a minority group in Buddhist Thailand, but just over the border in Malaya itself it was their own race that was to rule. It was the Sultans of Malaya who would be the rulers, once the Communists had been finally quelled, the British had withdrawn, and the country had gained its independence! And although most of the easy-going Malay peasants knew little and cared less for such things, there were those among them whose spirit had been fiercely inflamed, and who asserted bitterly that the four southern provinces of Thailand rightly belonged to the Malay people, from whom they had been wrested by the Thai hundreds of years ago. Some of them had already formed themselves into rebel bands and were lurking in the jungle-clad mountains of the borderland.

However, they were not to be confused with the Communist guerrillas, mainly Chinese, from Malaya, who were finding a refuge in those same mountains, using similar methods for different aims. Nor with the gentlemen smugglers who had ways and means of getting contraband goods across the border for purely mercenary motives. Nor with the law-breakers who had something to gain and nothing to lose by doing the dirtier work involved in the various political or economic enterprises of the border area. Nor with the individuals who saw ways of taking advantage of the general unrest to augment their incomes by a little skilful banditry here and there. The various groups went about their business with a suspicious and baleful eye on each other's activities, leading to periodical shoot-ups

between themselves. Expediency, however, sometimes demanded a measure of co-operation between them, particularly when it came to outwitting their common foe, the
Thai Government. The sunny south was not so peaceful as
it appeared on the surface, and the missionary team in Yala
soon realised that to the difficulties they must expect to
encounter might be added the dangers associated with what
were politely referred to as 'family feuds'.

'If it isn't one thing it's another!' they observed philo-
sophically. There had been plenty of bandits in China, and
guerrillas too, ravaging the countryside to add to the
horrors of the Sino-Japanese war. And afterwards the
Communist take-over had held terrors of its own, the
memories of which were still fresh. Yet over those last two
turbulent decades since the martyrdom of John and Betty
Stam in 1935, the only member of the Mission to meet with
death by violence had been one who was shot at close range
when a burglar broke into his office. The hundreds who had
been interned in Japanese camps, including children, had
emerged sound in life and limb, and in that very year of
1953, when the CIM officially commenced work in South
Thailand, the last two missionaries who had been held by
the Communists in China crossed safely over 'Freedom
Bridge' into Hong Kong.

It is true that one catastrophe in the same year had
startled the whole Mission, when the Comet in which the
British Home Director, Mr Fred Mitchell, was travelling
back from a visit to southeast Asia crashed in India, leaving
no survivors. The impermanent, uncertain quality of mortal
existence had been highlighted by this utterly unexpected
death of one in the prime of life on a normal, peaceful
mission when so many, apparently in great peril, had
escaped unharmed. Whether you took the view that in
matters of life and death, time and chance took a hand, or
that the whole affair was a spiritual conflict in which man's
reactions were deeply involved, or that God was supremely

in control and none could stay His Hand, made no funda-
mental difference to your personal duty in the light of your
calling. The reminder of that self-evident fact could only
encourage the team in Yala to stick it out, bandits or no
bandits. The dangers of the situation, in fact, were regarded
as minimal compared with the difficulties of learning two
new languages at once and making decisions regarding how
and where to extend evangelistic activities most effectively.

'Yala's on the railway, and the obvious place as our
centre of communications. Up the line to Bangkok, down
the line to Singapore!' they agreed. 'But it's not the best
centre for reaching the Malays.' So they went exploring and
made enquiries.

There were only two main roads out of Yala. One led
north-east to Pattani, the ancient capital, from where the
coast road ran for sixty miles south to Narathiwat, the port
where ships from Bangkok and Singapore called in periodically, and sea traffic across the Gulf of Thailand linked it
with Saigon.

The other road went south through rather hilly country
to the town of Raman, then down to Betong on the Malayan
border. It was called the Raman road. People seemed rather
averse to using it. 'There's nothing much on that road,' the
missionaries were told. 'It's rather lonely there . . . Too near
the jungle . . .'

But they did not want to go to Raman. By common consent they turned their attention to the coast road, where the
rich alluvial plains had drawn the people to wrest a living
from the soil as well as from the sea. It ran through paddy
fields and plantations, with views of luxuriant jungle-clad
hills in the distance. Little Malay kampongs, clusters of
houses of split bamboo raised from the ground on stilts,
were scattered along the dirt tracks and lanes leading off
the main highway. Some of those side roads ran towards
the coast, providing tantalising glimpses of a glittering blue
sea seen through the coconut palms fringing the shores.

Here and there the highway passed through a large village with open-fronted shops and cafés, and street vendors with rush mats on which their fruit and vegetables, rice and dried fish were spread. These were the local markets, and some of them were to figure very prominently in plans and activities later on. But in the early part of 1953 they were just unfamiliar names of places the Yala team passed by on the way to Pattani, then down to Narathiwat, Yaring, Pujud, Palas, Saiburi, Yingo . . .

As the year progressed, however, it was the market town of Saiburi that came into focus.

The initial entry into South Thailand by that team of four had been with a conviction that God was leading them there, and that He had a plan. No promise could be made by the Mission that reinforcements would be sent to them, and sometimes they felt they were behaving in rather a haphazard manner, going out sporadically to distribute tracts, trying to pick up phrases in two new languages at the same time, conscious often they were making silly mistakes. Yet beneath it all they knew they were gathering a basis of knowledge and experience they could pass on to younger workers, and as the year progressed they were heartened by the knowledge that their prayers to the Lord of the harvest were being answered. Others were preparing to join them, the labourers for whom they had prayed, and among them were doctors and nurses, eager to serve with their skills the people God had called them to.

Talks with Thai officials had revealed that a medical service for the rural areas would be acceptable, though it was unnecessary in towns like Yala, Pattani and Narathiwat, where hospitals and medical programmes were already adequate. A medical service! That would be in keeping with CIM tradition, whose young founder, Hudson Taylor, at the outset of his courageous enterprise of opening inland China to the proclamation of the Gospel, had rented an inconspicuous house in a Chinese city and in it sandwiched the dispensing of medicines with the preaching of the Jesus

Way. It had been a small beginning but it had led to great things, and set a pattern for pioneer work still worth following. That is why the market of Saiburi came into focus as the Yala team laboriously pursued their studies and their investigations. It was half-way between Pattani and Narathiwat on the coast road, and not much further from Yala though more difficult of access. What better situation for the centre of a rural medical service in the neglected southernmost tip of Thailand?

There was no time to be lost. 'The task is urgent,' wrote the leader of the team, well aware of the state of emergency in neighbouring Malaya, and the collapsing of the French colonial system in Indo-China, just across the water. 'It would seem that God is holding open the door in south-east Asia in order that His great purpose of bringing "many sons to glory" "of every tribe, and tongue, and people and nation", might be fulfilled. He is saying to Islam, the power that dominates South Thailand, "keep not back".' And because no words of his own could express the depth of the disquiet on his spirit sometimes when he thought about the Muslims, he concluded,

> Oft when the Word is on me to deliver
>   Lifts the illusion and the truth lies bare ...
> Then with a rush the intolerable craving
>   Shivers through me like a trumpet-call,
> Oh to save these! to perish for their saving,
>   Die for their life, be offered for them all.

Did some prophetic instinct tell him that in South Thailand, as in many other places down through the centuries, the delivering of the Word was to be accompanied by the ultimate offering?

His little booklet, containing information about South Thailand, was published in 1954, and already three doctors who had been in China were preparing to come to open medical work. They had first to learn sufficient Thai to do so, however, and were gaining experience in Presbyterian hospitals elsewhere in the country. Meanwhile, it was decided that the team in Yala should break up to gain footholds in other places. Seventy-year-old Mr G. K. Harris and his wife changed their minds about retirement after forty years in China and elected to return from Canada, to settle among Malays in the provincial capital of Pattani. The youngest member of the team, Doris Briscoe, went with a newly-arrived worker from Canada to live in a little wooden house on stilts in a Malay kampong on the outskirts of Narathiwat. And Dorothy Jupp, known to her colleagues as Juppy, settled with another new worker in one of the open-fronted shops on the road that passed through Saiburi.

With Bible pictures adorning the plain walls, a couple of tables and a few chairs, the shop was transformed into a guest room into which neighbours and their children wandered freely, and from which a good view could be obtained of the various means of transport that passed along the road. There were buses with passengers and freight mixed indiscriminately, inside and out; jeeps; bicycles, trishaws; buffaloes, and the occasional elephant.

Although Juppy was a midwife, and her companion a nurse, it was not until 1955 that the shop-house changed its character with the addition of two or three rooms, to become officially known as the Saiburi Christian Clinic with fully qualified doctors in attendance. It was opened with a flourish on 5th April, at a ceremony attended by a number of local officials and some personal friends of the missionaries, including an Indian doctor from Pattani accompanied by a Sikh merchant and a Chinese compradore. This international trio brought with them a generous gift of stools and chairs for the clinic, and also some wise advice, given out of their superior understanding of Thai customs and etiquette. This was promptly acted upon. The result was that a swift re-arrangement of furniture and a readjustment of personnel ensured it was the Chief of Police, and not a lesser mortal, who occupied the seat of honour. As he had been deputed to represent the Provincial Governor, it was just as well.

'Without exception the guests emphasised the complete lack of medical service in Saiburi and stated that the nearest doctors were fifty kilometres away, over difficult roads,' reported one of the Mission directors who had travelled up from Singapore to attend the ceremony. 'Their welcome seemed unaffected by repeated statements that we had come to preach the Gospel as well as to heal the sick.' Then he added, 'Ishmael, a Malay Muslim, is the registrar at the clinic.'

The significance of that simple statement was evident to those who understood the local situation, though it may have been surprising to those who did not. The employment of a Malay in the position of registrar was imperative if the Malays were to come to the clinic, for none of the missionaries knew the language well enough to deal with all the complicated questions and explanations that would inevitably arise. And since there was not one Malay in the whole of South Thailand who was not a Muslim, there was no alternative but to employ one who was.

So the medical work got under way, and with cautious optimism the doctors started to talk about building a hospital, similar, if smaller, to the one already opened at Manorom, in the central provinces. They looked around for a suitable site, and eventually decided to lease a plot of land on which to build at River Mouth, about a mile out of Saiburi along a shady lane leading to a picturesque lagoon.

Malaya gained its independence that same year. The Communist guerrilla forces had been firmly flushed out of the jungle at last, though it was rumoured many of them were lurking in the wild hilly country of the Thai border. Things were not getting any quieter there, nor the Malay separatists any less ambitious. Nor the smugglers any less greedy. Nor the 'family feuds' any less frequent. So there was usually a living of sorts to be made in the jungle for

criminals on the run, providing they were prepared to
rough it—and risk it.

The underworld activities and political intrigues about
which the missionaries read in the *Bangkok Post* and the
Voice of the Nation, and heard in conversations in the markets, were too complicated to fathom, and no business of
theirs, anyway. It was not for them to entangle themselves
with such affairs by ill-advised comment. They were living in
Thailand by courtesy of the government of the country, for
the purpose of proclaiming by word and deed a heavenly
kingdom, not an earthly one. This was their job, and if it involved some hazards, they were no greater than those facing
the people among whom they lived. So they agreed that the
old adage of 'least said, soonest mended' applied to border
politics and 'family feuds', and got on with their language
study, and tending the sick, and explaining the meaning of
their Bible pictures.

Bible pictures were their chief aids in telling the Gospel
to the Malays in those days. Even if they had had a wide
range of books and booklets and posters in the language,
as in Thai, they would have been of little use, since the vast
majority of the Malays coming to the clinic could not read.
And since there were no Malay Christians to do any of the
preaching, or whose voices could be recorded for reproduc-
tion on tape recorders, the most effective way to augment
the limited vocabulary and halting delivery of the missionaries remained that which had been used in China for
decades—pictures.

There was one picture in particular that provoked amazement and horror, argument and questioning. It was the
picture of the crucifixion of Jesus Christ.

'Ee! Why did they do that to Him?' asked the ignorant.

'If He had been a good man He wouldn't have had to
suffer like that,' argued the moralists, adding, 'God wouldn't
have let that happen to Him if He'd been a good man.'

'That never happened! He wasn't crucified at all!' asserted the Islamic teachers vehemently. 'The Koran says so. God took Him up to Heaven instead. He didn't die. That picture's wrong!'

That to save others He could not save Himself was beyond their comprehension, so the cross became the focal point, and the stumbling block.

'Herewith the first news of one for whom you are praying. Thank you very much for your prayers. The Lord wonderfully helped me through those last busy days. His strength enabled me to keep on rejoicing during the moments of saying goodbye to so many who have become so very dear to me.' Minka Hanskamp was writing her first letter to the group of friends in New Zealand who had pledged themselves to pray for her daily. She was travelling towards Singapore on the m.v. *Sydney*, one of a group of young missionaries from New Zealand and Australia, and her heart was full of joy as she briefly recounted the experiences of the journey. 'When we were together for prayer or just for a chat we could do nothing else but tell each other how we felt the Lord so very near . . .' On their arrival at Sydney they were met by a member of the Mission who took charge of them, and of their luggage. They could leave it all to him, he said.

'He is used to this work and in less than an hour our luggage had passed through the Customs and we were on our way to the Mission Home. Now we realised what was meant by so many of the people we met saying "The CIM is one big family." It was a thrill just to be taken into the family.' The new workers had a full programme of meetings to attend, interspersed with sightseeing, which included a visit to the Blue Mountains, but the highlight of it all to Minka was the prayer meeting which concluded with the celebration of the Lord's Supper. 'Most of those who were there had been on the field. I cannot describe how

wonderful this was—to be allowed to obey the Lord's command with people who had been serving Him for so many
years. It is wonderful to be allowed to be the Lord's.' They
had loosed away from Sydney to the sound of a crowd of
friends on the quay singing 'The Lord's my Shepherd', and
now, on the last lap of the journey, Minka was looking forward to what lay ahead. She summarised her desires in three
requests for prayer, and this is what they were:

'... That our lives may be real sermons.

'... That the Lord may clearly show the Directors and us
the countries in which He has work for us.

'... That we may be faithful, as He is always faithful.'

They arrived in Singapore on Sunday morning, 20th April
1958. On Monday 21st they had interviews with the Directors of the Mission, to discuss the all-important matter of
where they should be designated. There were seven or eight
countries in East Asia in which the Mission had centres of
work, and one of them was Indonesia. This had been one of
the main attractions for Minka when she was first drawn to
CIM, and her hope had been to go back to Java, the land of
her childhood and teenage memories. Even the horrors of
the internment camp had not spoiled the thought of it for
her. She knew the people, the climate, the customs, and it
would not mean another readjustment to a new country and
culture, as had been entailed in going to Holland and then
to New Zealand. However, missionary societies that had
previously not had workers in Indonesia were not finding it
easy to gain an entry, and Dutch people were particularly
unpopular. Even before she had her interview with the
Director she knew that this door was closed to her, and the
interview only served to confirm this. But to which of the
other countries was the door to open? Japan, Taiwan,
Philippines, Hong Kong, Malaya, Thailand, Laos ...

Tuesday was a day spent in much prayer, for final desig-
nations were to be made on Wednesday, and for Minka it
was a day when the thought of the little medical team in
South Thailand became fixed in her mind, and with it a

desire to join them. They were working among Malays, of
the same race as the Indonesians and the same religion. So
when, on Wednesday, the Director asked her if she would
be happy to go to South Thailand, as that was the place he
believed she was especially suited for, she responded eagerly.
The Lord had put into her heart a desire for the very place
to which her leader was designating her! It was a confirmation of the guidance the Lord had given her, she wrote ex-
citedly to her mother, saying it gave her great confidence
that she was in His will.

Minka was one to whom dates held a special significance,
whether connected with herself or others. People she had
met in all sorts of places were surprised and touched when
on a birthday or some other anniversary they received an
unexpected greetings card or a present from Minka to com-
memorate the occasion. So this date, 23rd April, was unforgettable, the day on which she was conscious that the One
Who claimed, 'I am He that openeth, and no man shutteth'
was holding open the door for her to pass to her life's work
in South Thailand.

In the language school in Singapore she was one of a
group of about thirty new workers, young men and women
from the United Kingdom and Europe, North America,
Australia and New Zealand, with varying temperaments
and backgrounds, but united right from the start of their
time together by two things—their allegiance to the Lord
Jesus Christ, and their conviction that He had led them to
East Asia with the CIM Overseas Missionary Fellowship.
There were some vigorous and sparkling personalities
among them, and the impression gained of Minka was of a
tall young woman with prematurely silvering hair, who kept
in the background and let others do most of the talking. She
was gentle and unusually considerate of others. When her
turn came in the fellowship meetings to tell her story, she
did so in a stark, unembellished way which made it all the
more arresting.

Brought up in Indonesia. Two and a half years at school

in Holland. Back to Indonesia at outbreak of the Second
World War. 'I could not get out then. One year later I was
saved through studying the catechism.'

Concentration camp. The miracle of the provision of
fresh vegetables and meat when her mother was seriously
ill. But during those years the question was in her mind:
'Why is there so much hate and grief'—but the Lord gave
no answer.

Family re-united, returned to Holland. 'We got a house
together, which was amazing. The Lord taught me many
things.' She hoped to be a midwife, but was delayed because
the quota was full. Three years training, two years nursing.
Then what? 'Should I go back to Java? But I never got
there. Should I go to New Zealand?' Her mother prayed
that she would get there, and her papers were ready in ten
weeks, instead of the usual wait of two years.

Her first year was not easy. 'That foreigner!' But later
she became a district midwife and was happy in this work.
Then the Lord took the joy away. Why?

'Sell all that thou hast and give to the poor and come,
follow Me.' She gave all her money, but it did not work. No
peace until she said, 'Here am I, send me.' She had been
homesick and booked a passage to Holland for February
13th—but instead, on February 12th, she went to Bible
College . . .!

She was glad when she had said it all, and could sit down.
She never found public speaking easy. She knew that as a
missionary she must be prepared to stand up and preach
and be stared at, but it was a relief to know that, as a nurse,
she would not have to do it often.

One of her inner experiences in Singapore she could only
share with those who would understand. She met a Japanese
girl. It was the first time she had met one of that race since
the concentration camp years with their dreaded Japanese
guards, and she was comforted at her own reaction. 'I had
no hate in my heart,' she told her mother thankfully. 'No

hate for her at all.' This peace instead of natural hatred was something she had experienced before in Java, when the war was over but Dutch nationals were still confined to the internment camps, for fear of Indonesian rebels. One young Indonesian terrorist had entered the camp where she was, and looking through a window had seen a Dutchman shaving himself before a mirror. The young terrorist had deliberately shot him dead, then in the ensuing uproar he himself had received a shot in the leg. He was taken into the camp hospital where Minka was nursing, and it fell to her lot to tend him. Her bitter anger as she thought of the ruthless murder of her fellow countryman, so recently re-united with his wife after the years of suffering and separation, subsided when she saw the young assailant with his leg shattered. With calm and even compassion she was able to nurse him. These inner experiences were too intimate and precious to be spoken of lightly, but to her were convincing evidence that the love of God was in control in her heart.

She had been aware of the need for that love in the internment camp itself. To forgive one's enemies was implicit in the teaching of Christ, and obedience was put to the test there.

'What are you doing?' she demanded once as she found her mother smacking little John severely for having allowed a Japanese guard to carry him around on his shoulders. The child must be taught to have nothing to do with these enemies! 'What are you doing? The man may have children of his own at home, and be missing them. We must pray for you,' Minka continued, looking at her mother reproachfully. 'We must pray that God will forgive you for what you have done.'

Forgiveness. It had to go deep. Only God's love in the heart could produce it. That was one of the things Minka had learned.

After the period for language study in Singapore she left for South Thailand, travelling by train with an English nurse who had been designated to the same field. A day and a night in the 'Golden Blowpipe' through the rice-fields and rich green Malayan jungle brought them to the Thai border, then a few more hours and they were in Yala, with its sounds and its sights and its smells that were strangely reminiscent of Java. The day started with the cry of the muezzin from the nearby mosque, followed by the sing-song calls of the street vendors, the hum of voices in the market, the monotonous twanging of string instruments in the evening, the barking of the street dogs in the deserted streets as the moon rode high. The sounds of the West had penetrated, too, with the back-firing of motor-bikes and the impatient toots of horns, radios blaring, and the loud speaker announcing *David and Bathsheba* on show twice nightly at the cinema. The smell of kerosene exhaust gas pervaded the bus station as well as the rich odour of spices from the food shops, the fresh smell of fruit and vegetables and dried fish in the market, and the acrid stench of open drains. Skirts and shorts mingled with sarongs, plastic bags with hand-woven baskets, jeeps with the occasional elephant. But Yala was an eastern city and its inhabitants the people of the east, where life is lived in the street, everybody knows everybody else's business, and man is not shut off from his neighbour by the isolation of the closed front door. To some of the new missionaries it came as rather a shock to see a man brushing his teeth in the street, or a woman suckling her baby on a stool in her doorway, but to Minka there was nothing strange about it. It was just like the Java of her childhood.

Pattani, of course, was even more so, for there was no railway, and it was the cultural centre of the Malays of South Thailand. Minka lived here as one of a group of new workers for several months, in a wooden house in a Malay kampong, for it had been agreed that Malay should be her major language. With her previous knowledge of Javanese, in many ways similar to Malay, and her natural aptitude for languages, she made quicker progress than some of the others, and had she been of a different disposition she might have made things difficult for them. It was not unknown for younger workers in similar circumstances to take matters into their own hands when they realised their grasp of the language was superior to that of their seniors, to make decisions and take the lead as though they were the ones in charge. Minka never gave offence in that way. Indeed, her fault lay at the other extreme, for she deprecated herself and her own abilities to such a degree that her colleagues sometimes found themselves getting irritated as they tried in vain to convince her that she was a better Malay speaker than most of them, as good a midwife as any they'd ever known, that her Christian witness was a challenge to them all, that the way she preached was clear and convincing, and that there was no reason for her to be discouraged about herself . . .

'There's no good in Minka' was her unalterable conviction. Even the argument 'Minka, don't underestimate the gifts that God has given you!' failed to change her attitude. She could not believe that in anything she matched up to what she ought to be.

'When Minka stands before the Lord and He says to her "Well done, good and faithful servant", she'll look over her shoulder to see who He's talking to!' observed one of her fellow missionaries. 'Simply won't believe He's saying it to her!'

She would certainly have felt there was some mistake if she'd known what was in the private report sent by her Superintendent to the Directors in Singapore two years after she had arrived in south-east Asia. The only negative notes struck in the whole report were the observations that she had not as yet been successful in actually leading souls to Christ, and that she had difficulty with sleep if she were in noisy conditions. She got on well with her fellow missionaries and the local people, her influence was very helpful, she was most considerate and always put others first, was very humble, always cheerful, adaptable, dependable and diligent, her spiritual life was maintained, her patience was average, she had a fine spirit and would never give in, and altogether was a fine character who would make a most valuable worker.

Though she had not personally led any in Pattani to put their trust in Christ, the number of people attending the Sunday services, mainly Chinese, had increased during the eighteen months she was there from two or three to nearly twenty. Suspicion had been broken down among the Malay neighbours too, so that mothers no longer refused to allow their children to come to listen to Bible stories and sing Christian choruses. 'Now you can see them coming every Friday, sometimes a few, sometimes a dozen or more,' wrote Minka, and reported thankfully that she was making progress with the language. 'When I came the only thing I could give as an answer to people who tried to talk to me was smiles. Of course it is still difficult, but it was with a grateful heart that I experienced that the children had understood the story I told them when I took the children's meeting for the first time. The Lord gave me also some opportunities to tell to people who wandered in the meaning of some of the posters which hang in the guest room.'

She was definite in her prayers when embarking on some piece of service. The little group of women missionaries had decided they would go to the Malay market and offer books for sale—Gospels and other portions of Scripture. They set out with some trepidation, for they knew they might encounter opposition from fanatical Muslims, but Minka had already made her petition. 'I asked the Lord to be allowed to sell thirty sets of books. We sold at least thirty-five sets and some other books, mostly to Malays. At first they were scared even to touch the books, but again the Lord heard us, and one after the other came and bought— even some of the pupils of the mosque school. Again we saw how the Master answered abundantly.'

Her time in the house in the Malay kampong was drawing to a close, however, for the building of the hospital by the lagoon a mile from Saiburi town was nearly completed and the official date of opening was 1st January, 1960. Minka was to be one of the nurses, and early in December she moved from Pattani to the place that for the next ten years was to be her home and the centre of her life.

CHAPTER FOUR

ANYWHERE FOR GOD

From Margaret Morgan's notebook

Be still My child
and listen while I talk with you.
Be still and listen for My voice
My voice is quiet and restful
not raucous and loud.
　　My voice speaks within your being
You must be still and hear it
attentive to what I have to say
expecting that I will speak.

Be still My child
and listen to My voice.
Mine is the voice of authority
of command
of comfort
of consolation
My voice reassures,
revives,
restores,
and brings rest of heart.
Listen for it My child
I would have you learn from Me.
　　　　　　　　　　　　M.M.

When she was tempted to act too quickly

'BANDITS IN THAILAND would take a great fancy to that green bag of yours, I should think!' said Mr Morgan with a twinkle in his eye. 'Better leave it behind if you go there!' There was a chuckle from Mum, a giggle from Elaine, and Margaret, who had just arrived home for a couple of days, fresh and crisp as always, smiled and glanced down at the handbag hanging over her arm. It blended perfectly with her ensemble. Margaret's bag and gloves and scarves were all carefully chosen, the colours matching and blending or skilfully contrasting, but this particular bag was very distinctive. 'You'll be asking for trouble if you take that with you.'

'Perhaps you're right,' agreed Margaret easily, putting it down and taking off her gloves. 'How are you, Dad?' She gave him a quick glance as she spoke. Dad had not been well lately. Among other things he had angina, and this knowledge brought Margaret home more frequently than usual. It was a factor in preventing her taking any definite step towards applying for Bible College training. If Dad were ill and Mum needed her, she knew she would have no peace of mind unless she were free to be with them. But the thought of missionary work overseas was increasingly with her in this year of 1960, and her family sensed it.

It had been implanted in her mind when she attended the Keswick Convention in the Lake District one year. She had just completed her nursing and midwifery training at the time, and was looking forward to getting a wide and varied experience in her chosen profession. She was only twenty-two, and there was plenty of time yet before she need make decisions regarding what might or might not have been a divine call to missionary work in her teens. She wasn't really too sure about it. But by the time the week's convention was over she had come to a new stage in her spiritual life. It was very simply expressed in her own words, 'I was willing to go anywhere for God.' When a friend of hers said, some time later, 'Perhaps the Lord wants you to be a missionary, Margaret,' she knew that the deep impression received in the great tent at the Keswick Convention was being confirmed, for people were not in the habit of speaking to her like that. The general impression was that she was far too delicate for such a life. Fired with the desire to move out at once into the pathway God seemed to be directing for her, she had set about making application to go to Bible College. This seemed a necessary preliminary to offering herself as a missionary somewhere or other—where she had not the slightest idea.

It was at this point that she became uneasy. 'I had no peace about it,' she explained later, and then a sentence from a verse in Isaiah came to her with the indefinable significance that she recognised was God's Spirit speaking directly to her. 'Ye shall not go out with haste . . .'

The words were so simple and the message so clear she had no doubt as to their meaning. She was being restrained in her eagerness to embark immediately on a missionary career. She took no further steps about applying to a Bible College, but continued with her nursing. She was conscious, though, that she was merely being delayed, not stopped altogether, and that when the right time came she would be shown what to do. The years that followed tested her patience and her purpose, but they also clarified the path she was to tread. More and more it was towards Thailand that she looked.

Her interest in that country was born out of her friendship with Brenda Holton with whom she had kept in touch after they both left Bristol. Brenda, having completed her general nursing and midwifery training, had gone to Bible College and then applied to the CIM Overseas Missionary Fellowship. It was as one of the accepted candidates who were preparing to set out for the Far East that she invited Margaret to attend the Easter conference at Swanwick in Derbyshire. In the pleasantly-situated conference centre some three hundred people gathered to hear about and pray about proclaiming the Gospel and making disciples in the countries of south-east Asia. This was primarily a spiritual enterprise, it was affirmed, and the need for adequate spiritual resources was emphasised, people who would stand behind the work and the workers in persistent, believing prayer. 'Prayer Companions' were those who undertook to pray daily for a specific missionary, and the missionary in turn would periodically write letters giving information about the progress of the work and matters needing special intercession. It was a solemn committal of partnership in the spiritual realm, and when Margaret linked up as a Prayer Companion to Brenda Holton she took it seriously. The quarterly letters that Brenda sent were read carefully, her movements followed with interest, the requests for prayer faithfully observed. When Brenda went to Thailand Margaret's thoughts, naturally enough, often went there, and gradually the conviction was born that it was the country to which God would lead her, too.

A book entitled *Fierce the Conflict* served to deepen the conviction, though it brought her face to face with the risks that might be involved. The book was the story of Lilian Hamer, a missionary nurse who had been robbed and murdered on a lonely trail on the northern borders of Thailand in the same month that Brenda had set out for the Far East. Reading it had moved Margaret very much, as her family noticed. They had all read the book when Dad made his laughing remark about the green handbag, and their light-hearted reactions indicated that they knew in which direction her thoughts for the future were veering. But it is doubtful whether they seriously believed she would get there. Margaret was an ardent supporter of missions and reader of the CIM books and magazine, and that was a role that suited her very well. Missionaries needed supporters at home, and robust health was not necessary to fulfil that obligation. To go abroad to the rigours of living in a trying climate and in primitive conditions was quite a different matter. Margaret might dream about it, but that was as far as it was likely to get.

But later that year Dad died, and when Mum and Elaine had readjusted their lives to being without the tall, good-looking father of the home, with his kindliness and his humour, and his love of books, and when Margaret had got over the grief of losing him, she realised that there was now no valid reason why she should not go forward on what she believed to be the path God was directing her into. Her decision to do so was met with dismay.

'Oh, Marg! Two years at Bible College?' Elaine asked sadly. It had been bad enough to a little girl's way of thinking when her big sister went away to Bristol and only came back once a fortnight. It had been even worse when her midwifery training took her away for six months. But now, to be going to faraway London for two years! At fourteen years of age Elaine could look no further ahead than that. A separation of two years seemed like a lifetime. But Mrs Morgan looked further. She realised now that the determination and tenacity underneath Margaret's gentleness which had brought her through her nursing training would probably prove sufficient to get her to the Far East. But would they be sufficient to overcome the limitations of her physical weaknesses? Mrs Morgan was apprehensive, and said so, knowing however that her arguments would be unavailing.

So Margaret went to Mount Hermon Missionary Training College for women in Ealing, and the first time she faced the ordeal of speaking to the assembled company she based her talk on the words, 'He that waiteth on the Lord shall not make haste'. She could speak from experience, for it was five years since she had committed herself at Keswick to go anywhere for God.

During that time, however, one thing had become fixed in her mind. She knew where she was going, and she knew with which society. She was preparing to go to the Far East with the CIM Overseas Missionary Fellowship, and she felt it would be to Thailand.

'Whatever *shall* I do if CIM won't accept me?' she exclaimed in sudden alarm once to a fellow student heading for Africa, as they spoke about the societies to which they were applying. She had no alternative plan if it was decided she was unsuitable. Any other future was inconceivable.

Her fear that she would not be accepted, however, proved groundless. The waiting time was over now, and things moved forward quietly and steadily. She was already in touch with the Candidates Secretary of the Mission and had filled in her application papers outlining her personal faith and experience. When she had completed her two years at Mount Hermon she was invited to attend the Candidates' Course at the mission's London headquarters, at the end of which it would be decided whether her offer of service should be accepted or not. She arrived as one of a group of a dozen young people one day in October 1963.

The purpose of the Candidates' Course was simple enough. It provided the Mission officers with the opportunity to assess the physical, mental and spiritual calibre of the candidates, and the candidates with the opportunity of seeing the Mission 'from the inside'. Intermingled with lectures of a general nature were intimate talks and unconscious practical evidences of the character of the Mission, its financial policy, its aims and methods of work, and above all its relationship to God.

It was evangelical, as they all knew. That was why they had applied. The papers they had filled in had given evidence of their own convictions regarding the inspiration of the Scriptures, the fall of man, the atoning death of Christ, the resurrection of the body, the eternal life of those who were justified by faith, and the eternally lost condition of those who were not. It was mainly on the basis of what they had written in those doctrinal papers that they were here at all.

It was also evangelistic. It regarded the winning of men to Christ, the building up of believers in the faith and integrating them with other believers into local churches as its primary objective. Its claim to being international and interdenominational was justified by the fact that its General Director happened to be a Baptist from New Zealand, and his predecessor an Anglican bishop from Britain. As for its financial policy,

'The Mission is supported by God through the free-will offerings of His people. The needs of the work are laid before God in prayer, and no person is authorised to solicit funds on behalf of the Mission.' That was what it said in the *Principles and Practices*, the candidates were told. 'You will find everything clearly outlined there. It is a very important document, and you will be required to sign it when and if you become a member of the Mission. You should all read it and study it, because if you do not cordially approve of what is written in it, and intend to act on these principles, you'd better withdraw your application now . . .'

So they all read it, and inevitably certain phrases struck a deep chord in their minds.

'Candidates are expected to have a sense of divine call and to show evidence of it.'

'Every member should recognise that his dependence for the supply of all his need is not in the human organisation, but upon God who called him and whom he serves. Although funds might fail, or the Mission cease to exist, yet if the members put their trust in Him He will never fail nor disappoint them.'

'Every member of the Mission must fully understand that he depends for help and protection on the living God and does not rely on any human authority . . . Those engaged in the Lord's work should be prepared to take joyfully the spoiling of their goods and to rejoice that they are counted worthy to suffer shame for His name.'

The document concluded with some words of Hudson Taylor, the founder, who for all that he was a Victorian had a pungent way of saying things, devoid of flowery phrases.

'If the members are godly and wise, walking in the spirit of unity and love, they will not lack divine guidance in important matters and at critical times; but should another spirit prevail, no rules could save the Mission, nor would it be worth saving. The China Inland Mission must be a living body in fellowship with God, or it will be of no further use, and cannot continue.'

There was nothing emotional about the wording of *Principles and Practice*, and there was nothing emotional about the conduct of affairs at the Mission's headquarters in the rather down-at-heel neighbourhood in North London known as Newington Green. The offices opened at nine in the morning and closed at five in the evening, there was a prayer meeting for half an hour in the Mission Home to which all might go, and a midday meal in the dining room, when everybody crowded in to sit at random around the long tables with a minimum of formality, the youngest typist taking a vacant seat beside the Home Director without embarrassment. Once a week there was a prayer meeting held for thirty minutes before the tea break which only members of the Mission were expected to attend, and this was the only occasion when there were any public references made to financial needs. Apart from that, and from the card pinned on the noticeboard each day announcing the amount received in donations, money or the lack of it seemed rarely to be mentioned.

The matter came up occasionally in informal conversations when the Candidates Secretary, Mr Leslie Lyall, recounted experiences of money coming to him and his wife out of the blue—as, for example, when they were booked to cross the Pacific en route for China with their four children on a military transport in 1946. After heavy baggage had been forwarded they had nothing in hand to pay for all incidentals, which included food on the railway journey from Vancouver to San Francisco, luggage handling costs and tips on board ship. Yet they saw all needs met at each step of the journey to Shanghai. 'The Lord always provides,' they said. 'Even when we were in a beleaguered city in China, all our neighbours having fled from the invading Japanese, and our third child only one day old . . . Money wouldn't have been much use then, even if we'd had it— but the chicken that flew over the wall from who knows where provided just the nourishing broth the baby's mother was needing!'

The atmosphere of the place was cheerful and business-like, and there was a sense of purposefulness about what went on. The candidates, by and large, liked what they saw, approved the 'P and P', and hoped they would be accepted when the Council met to decide their future. They looked forward with varying degrees of apprehension, buoyancy or confidence, according to temperament, to the occasion when one by one they must appear before the august body and answer up for themselves. Margaret, naturally of a rather timid disposition, was thankful when her turn was over, although everyone endeavoured to put her at her ease, and the only questions asked were those she could readily answer.

Her case presented no problems. It was pointed out that she was of average ability, with no outstanding qualifications or experience, but that she had qualities of character that were likely to wear well. She was quiet and unassuming, but efficient, practical, trustworthy and thoughtful. She was rather diffident, but when given responsibility shouldered it with composure. She was healthy, though possibly tired easily. Her aunt, Miss Florence Eynon, a member of the Mission for about forty years and one of her referees, had had no hesitation in recommending Margaret, except on that one point. 'My only anxiety is that she should not be strong enough physically, and overwork.'

There was not much more to report. She had made good grades at the Wycliffe School of Linguistics during the summer, and had been co-driver in a party of twelve who went for a five weeks' tour across Europe to Israel. As for her evangelical faith and conviction, there was no doubt of her soundness and sincerity, nor that she had applied to the Mission because she believed God had led her to do so. She was prepared to go anywhere—hers was an open offer—but would like to make use of her nursing training, and would prefer village clinic work to hospital nursing. She was the type to fit easily into the Mission fellowship, and make a reliable member of its rank and file.

'I'm glad to be able to tell you that the Council unanimously accepted your application to join the Mission,' she was told. 'You'll be flying out to Singapore with the party going in the Spring. We're glad you're joining us, Margaret . . .'

So it was as an accepted candidate of the CIM Overseas Missionary Fellowship that she returned to home in Porth for the Christmas holidays, and it was in that capacity she met Brenda Holton again. Brenda had been back in England on her first furlough for a few months, and now her itinerary of deputation meetings led her to Newport in South Wales. Margaret went along eagerly to see her, and the two girls spent an afternoon together.

That meeting somehow imprinted itself very deeply on Brenda's memory. Although she had written home to her prayer companions regularly, she was surprised at how much Margaret knew about the situation in South Thailand, and the points she raised. But there was something she perceived during the conversation which she had not expected.

'She was full of the most intelligent questions,' Brenda reported ten years later. 'It was amazing how much she understood about South Thailand and our work there. But some of the things she asked revealed—fear. She really was one who knew what it was to be afraid. As we talked that afternoon it showed—her fearful self.'

Brenda paused, her memory travelling swiftly over the
years she had known Margaret in Thailand. It had been
quickened by what she had found as she had been sorting
out the belongings of Minka and Margaret in the little
house in Pattani where they had lived. 'It is quite significant
to me to remember the first talk she ever prepared in Thai
was one entitled "Are You Afraid?" I found the notes of
this talk when I was packing up her things.' Brenda's voice
broke slightly as she spoke. The task of disposing of the
contents of that little house in Pattani had not been accomplished without emotion welling up from time to time. 'She
started off right at the beginning with the words, "Are you
afraid? Are you afraid of the bandits? Are you afraid of
sickness? Are you afraid of death? Are you afraid of the
spirits . . .?"'

Fear. It was a subject she knew something about. She
could understand people who were afraid.

'Margaret was that sort of person,' Brenda continued.
'She feared illness and difficult situations. But that didn't
mean she didn't face up to them. She faced up to them
all right . . .'

And that is surely the highest form of courage.

Perhaps, too, it explains why, when still at the Missionary
Training College Margaret went into a fellow student's room
one day, face radiant, and said:

'I've just been reading in the Amplified New Testament.
Listen, isn't this wonderful?' "God Himself has said, I will
not in any way fail you, nor give you up, nor leave you without support. I will not, I will not, I will not in any degree
leave you helpless, nor forsake you, nor let you down, nor
relax my hold on you . . ." Think of it, Jean! Never, no
never, no never . . .!'

In 1974, when Jean was working in a little inland town in
Brazil and heard that Margaret was being held captive by
bandits in Thailand, she remembered the radiant face and
the confident voice exclaiming. 'Never, no never, no
never . . .' That vivid mental picture was a help as she

prayed for her friend, for if she remembered, could the One who had made the promise possibly forget?

Although Margaret, on arrival at Singapore in April 1964, was designated to work in South Thailand, over a year was to elapse before she eventually arrived there. After the initial period in Singapore she was sent to the capital of Thailand, Bangkok, to the newly created Union Language Centre. Her acute hearing and her inherent love of music gave her an advantage in studying a tonal language, and this specialised course provided her with a correctness and facility in the Thai language which was the admiration and envy of fellow missionaries, many of whom never attained it. However, her private diary, which she kept only spasmodically, dealt with matters which to her were of far deeper significance than accomplishments in study. Half an hour spent with a fellow student in private prayer was the only event entered one day, with the observation, 'How gracious the Lord is to draw our hearts towards Himself! Feel the encouraging and urging of the Holy Spirit these days.' The following day the entry started with the words:

'Am I prepared to meet the Lord face to face? A challenging thought.' She had been reading the story of Roy Orpin, a young New Zealander who, the previous year, had been murdered on a North Thailand trail. Like Lilian Hamer he had been a member of the OMF*, and to Margaret, in the same country now and a member of the same Mission, the book was relevant and arresting. Her diary continued,

'Twice lately have come across that statement by John Dene, "one of these days you'll hear that J.D. has died. Don't you believe it! I'll be more alive than ever I was before!" It is a solemn thing, surely, in a man's life when

---

* The China Inland Mission was changed officially to Overseas Missionary Fellowship in 1965, one hundred years after the founding of the Mission.

he knows that his earthly journey is drawing to a close.'
Then she wrote on in that little private record, words she
thought no eyes but hers would ever see, 'Even so come,
Lord Jesus.'

During the long time of language study in Bangkok she
had several opportunities to visit OMF workers in the fertile plains of the central provinces, and it was here she had
her first experience in up-country evangelism. The weather
was very hot—'I have just thrown some cold water over
myself, thinking it might aid my concentration!'—and she
had gone to a small mission centre with a fellow student:

'. . . expecting that we would have a nice restful time. But
the Lord knew what we needed and planned otherwise. The
senior missionary had everything organised for us to go out
selling literature. We left the house at 8 o'clock on Saturday
morning armed each with a basket full of booklets, some to
give away and some to sell. At first I approached the Thai
homes with some trepidation and with a fervent prayer to
the Lord that He would bring some Thai words into my
mind! This is the first time I have done anything like this
in Thailand, and it really gave me much joy to be able to
serve the Lord in this small way. We went out again for
some hours in the evening doing the same thing in a different part of the town.'

The next day they went through the dusty streets to a little
house on stilts in which lived a woman with leprosy. Dogs
nosed around underneath it, chickens pecked on the ground,
and 'here we sat for two and a half hours on a small wooden
platform. We first had a service with a crowd of children
who came running eagerly as soon as they saw us arrive,
and then we had a time of fellowship with the Christian lady
herself.' She was being introduced to pioneer missionary
work in the east, with its dust and its heat and its flies, its
curious, straggling onlookers, its swarms of children. But
later on she began to learn what was involved in leaving the
town and going into the country.

'Did some visiting with Ruth. First day we went out for

miles, cycling to visit *two* people. Had not cycled for years. Both of us fell off twice within the first half an hour!' The rough, narrow tracks between the paddy fields were very different from the roads in Wales!

'We left at 2 p.m. and reached our first house out in the middle of nowhere about 3.30.

'She was out . . .!

'We then crossed a river standing up in a boat, bike and all! Got to our second poor little home at 4.15, and had a little service, tended to the patient's sores and gave her an injection. These visits were to invite the folk to a special leprosy gathering on the Sunday. We put our bikes on a bus for most of the return journey. Thought I'd never make it . . .' Margaret almost invariably got a headache after she had been out in the sun for an hour.

But when nineteen people with leprosy turned up for the special meeting on Sunday, and she listened to a Thai Christian preaching to them of Jesus Christ, and His death on the cross, and His resurrection, and what it all could mean to them, she could only report 'it was really inspiring'. Her up-country visit that time included visits to five leprosy clinics, thatched booths in rather out-of-the-way places, where the patients who tried to hide their disease could come unobserved to collect their medicine, receive their injections, and have their sores cleansed.

'One was at Wiset. Shirley and I went off by boat at 7 a.m. and got there at 1.30. Then we did some visiting and had a memorable ride—three of us on Jim Giblet's motorbike! Ruth joined us for the clinic on Tuesday, then we returned to Singburi and I left next morning, not wanting to leave one bit.' And that entry in her diary concluded with the words, 'Really feel the Lord is calling me into this type of work.'

She had affirmed while still in England that she felt drawn to working in clinics in country areas rather than to serving in a hospital. Now she had had the opportunity of trying it out, and in spite of the headaches and the dirt, and the not infrequent bouts of diarrhoea, the conviction persisted. It was to persist through several more years yet, for in South Thailand leprosy work had not even started. The hospital at Saiburi was still under-staffed, and Margaret knew she would be required there, for Brenda Holton had written recently in one of her letters to Prayer Companions, 'We are busier than ever, and because of further losses among the nurses, the hospital cannot release me for preparation for leprosy work this year.' Margaret knew they were waiting for her there, and that the addition of a fully qualified nurse and midwife who could also speak Thai would be a step towards releasing Brenda for the work she so clearly believed God was calling her to do.

Margaret arrived in South Thailand at the end of August 1965. Her thoughts had so often been there, she had studied pictures and slides of the place, read about it so much, that after she had been to the Sunday service, then gone along to report at the police station as was required, she said, 'I'm beginning to feel as if I have come home!' The appearance of Brenda a couple of evenings later, over from Saiburi to greet her, completed it. The Casualty Sister and the young nurse trainee who first met at the Bristol Royal Infirmary in 1952 had plenty to say to each other, and Margaret's diary for that day ended briefly:

'Brenda arrived evening. Good to natter. Went to bed late.'

CHAPTER FIVE

SHOULDER TO THE WHEEL

From Margaret Morgan's notebook

My child, hear My voice
Don't listen to that of another
Trust Me and allow Me to be your Guide.
I will direct and lead
but you must let Me be in control.
I love you very much
Remember the price I paid to redeem you.
Remember the cost involved
That is how much I care.
You must trust Me
even though the way seems dark at times.
Rest in Me, My child,
secure in the knowledge
of My care for you.
                              M.M.

When seeking guidance about furlough

BRENDA HOLTON LIFTED the box of medicines onto the rough table in an open-fronted shop at the crossroads in Palas market town, and started putting them out on a shelf. Enamel basins lay on the cement floor, and swabs and bandages in a plastic bag beside them. The Bible pictures were already hanging on the wall, and on a small table below one of them was a little pile of tracts.

She was preparing for the weekly leprosy clinic that had at last been opened in the market town half-way between Pattani and Saiburi, and already the patients were beginning to appear, sidling rather shamefacedly into the dimmest corners of the room. A woman in a bright sarong whose hairless brow and slightly swollen cheek betrayed the disease she longed to hide; a Thai man in a smart-looking suit, who had arrived in a taxi; a lad in a rather grubby sarong who limped in with a self-conscious, apologetic grin. They were coming, these people with leprosy whose need had somehow called to her when years ago she had heard missionaries on furlough from Central Thailand speak about the leprosy clinics that were being opened there. It was the most effective way of stopping the spread of the disease, those missionaries had asserted, now that new drugs were providing a door of hope for those who previously had none. Leprosy could be cured if taken in time, and the way to do it was to have regular clinics to which patients could come for their medicines and treatment, returning home to live normal

lives like anyone else. The day of the leprosarium with its
segregated population, its pathetic inmates who in most
cases had come there to die, was passing. The very word
leper was spoken no more—those who had the disease were
suffering from leprosy, just as some people suffered from
anaemia, and others from arthritis, or diphtheria or measles.
No stigma should be associated with it, no social ostracism
added to the sufferings of those who had contracted it. 'Heal
the sick' had been one of the commissions Christ had given
to his disciples, and even before she got to Thailand Brenda
had glimpsed in the rural clinics a simple way in which she
could help to fulfil that particular commission. So here she
was, in the summer of 1966, her main work no longer that
of a general nurse in the Christian Hospital at Saiburi, but
that of a leprosy nurse with responsibility for the weekly
clinics—one at Saiburi, one at the market town of Palas, and
one in the fishing village of Kampong Atas.

It looked like being a busy day, and her face lit up with
a smile as she saw a bicycle being propped up outside, and
a tall figure making its way towards her. 'Oh, Minka,' she
said. 'You've come again! I'm so glad!' Then she added, to
show her gratitude, 'But for you to give up every Wednesday, your free day, to come and help me . . .!'

'Oh, I love it!' replied Minka enthusiastically. 'I'd rather
be doing this than anything else. Should I start registering
the patients? No, wait a minute. I'll get you some water in
a basin for the boy over there to soak his foot. That's the
first thing,' and Minka was off, practical as always, seeing
what needed to be done and then doing it. Wednesday was
the best day of the week for her now, when she could get
away from the hospital with its schedules to observe and
its standards to maintain—standards that necessitated
keeping a vigilant eye on everything one was respon-
sible for, including one's own reactions when things
went against the grain. When, for instance, one was put
in charge of a group of Thai nurse aides whose language
one could not understand or speak correctly, Malay having

been the language one had been expected to concentrate on. Or when, coming off night duty and longing for sleep, the nurse in the next room, from whom one was separated by a flimsy partition through which every sound could be heard, suddenly started to type some letters, having forgotten one's presence. Or when a patient who came pleading his pathetic orphaned state and got away with a reduced rate on that account, later came in boasting that his father was making the pilgrimage to Mecca that year. That sort of thing was infuriating! The man was not only a liar, but a scrounger as well! Minka was indignant. She could not understand how the others, especially the English, could see a funny side to it. The years on the hospital staff at Saiburi had made fresh demands on her as she found herself once more having to readjust to new conditions and people from different countries, and there had been times when she had confided to one of the older missionaries that she felt she was being misjudged.

'Don't worry if people criticise you—just make sure it isn't justified,' was the wise advice given. 'If they're wrong, they'll come to see it. And if you're wrong,' her counsellor added with a twinkle in her eye, '*you'll* come to see it!' And Minka smiled. She could always react favourably to the voice of reason. It was the voice of authority that tended to put her on edge, as her colleagues observed, and gradually came to understand. 'It's the effect of those years of internment . . . the Japanese guards giving orders demanding unquestioning obedience . . . she reacts instinctively against authority . . .'

The effect of those years of internment was evident in other ways, too, noticeably in Minka's almost unnatural disregard for the needs of her own body. 'She eats like a sparrow!' people said, and when she explained that she'd been on a starvation diet so long that she was physically unable to digest much food at a time, they argued that in that case she ought to eat little, but often. But she was usually too busy with other matters to remember to do so, and perhaps that is why, on one occasion she was never allowed to forget, she was mistaken for a ghost.

The incident occurred shortly after the Saiburi Christian Hospital had been opened, and she was on night duty. As is the way in the East, patients did not come to hospital alone, but with at least one relative who was prepared to sleep anywhere, under the bed if necessary, so long as it was near enough to provide the company and companionship which all sick persons must surely need! There was no keeping them away, and the arrangement had its advantages, for patients got the food they liked, cooked in strict adherence to their personal preferences and religious beliefs. With Muslims who refused to eat pork, Thai with a taste for curry and Chinese who liked their food delicately spiced, to run a hospital kitchen to suit everybody would have required three different staffs and catering establishments. It was much simpler for patients to send out to the restaurant down the lane for what they wanted, or have it cooked for them in a corner of the compound by someone squatting beside an iron pot on a charcoal fire. By all means let the patient's friends and relations come to hospital, providing they were prepared to bed down somewhere where they would not completely obstruct the doctors and nurses in attending to their duties! Their presence ensured that in case of emergencies, there was always someone to call on.

An emergency occurred when Minka was on night duty. One of the patients died. It was unexpected, and sadly she went to break the news to the nearest relative, slumped over in sleep at the foot of the bed. He awakened suddenly to see bending over him a very long, very thin figure in white, with white hair, and lightish-coloured eyes looking straight at him out of a rather gaunt face. And the figure was speaking of death! With a gasp of horror he jumped to his feet, vaulted over the verandah, sped across the moonlit courtyard, and leaping over the fence disappeared into the coconut grove beyond. He was not discovered until hours later, when he returned to admit he was absolutely certain it was a ghost who had spoken to him.

'You see, Minka, you really *must* eat more!' And Minka, always ready to laugh when the joke was on her, laughed with them. But she continued to eat like a sparrow! She continued to drive her body, too, in spite of constantly recurring back trouble, and cycled when most people would have waited for a bus, or maybe wouldn't have gone at all. When it came to giving a helping hand in the leprosy work, nothing but hospital duty could stop her. So in that first memorable year Brenda, officially the only nurse designated to the leprosy clinic work, frequently found Minka alongside. It was with Minka alongside that she found Jit.

She heard about Jit very shortly after the clinic in Palas market had been opened. 'There's a boy with leprosy at Khuan,' she was told. 'He lives by himself. His family won't let him live with them. He never comes out of his little hut. He'll die soon. Perhaps if you went to see him ...?' So when all the patients had been attended to they set off for the mile walk on the side road that led to the village of Khuan. The sun was blazing down on them, and the short cut proved to be a narrow path across the rice fields, which ended in a stream. 'Just wade downstream till you get to the path on the left—see? Follow that up to the big house on stilts, and round by the side of it you'll find a little shack. Jit is in there.'

There they found him—a lad in his teens, crouching on a low bed in a sort of lean-to, amid a pile of old clothes, water pitchers and cooking pots on the ground beside him. They had to bend down to peer in, and saw him glowering up at them like an angry, suspicious animal. How could he know that these two pale-skinned western women whom he had never seen before were the answer to the inarticulate prayer that had been in his heart to the Someone he felt must somewhere exist, 'the great Person or power who held everything in his control,' as he expressed it years later. On that hot summer afternoon he only knew they were strangers who

had come to look at him, and it took some persuasion on
their part to convince him that they had medicine for him
that would heal him of his disease, if only he would take it
regularly, and follow the instructions they gave him.

After that first visit Brenda went regularly to take him his
medicine and dress his sores, and Minka whenever she was
able. He was one of many who were visited in that way, for
although sufferers from leprosy were not segregated, they
were shunned, and many of them could not be persuaded to
leave their homes to attend the clinics and face the obvious
contempt of those they met on the roads or in the markets.
So if they were to be healed, Brenda realised she must go
to them. Once patients were registered and had been started
on a course of treatment it was vitally necessary to keep
them on it, and ensure they were taking their medicine in
the right doses at the right times. The vast majority of them
were completely ignorant about the use of modern medicine, and were easily discouraged when they were not cured
almost overnight.

'I thought I'd be healed by now—I've taken your medicine
for a month!'

'But if one pill three times a day does me good, surely I'll
get better much quicker if I take three pills three times a
day?'

'I took them for two days and I wasn't any better, so I
stopped taking them. Why can't you give me an injection
strong enough to last until you come next time?'

The regular journeys to the out-of-the-way villages and
hamlets along the coast, where the highest incidence of
leprosy was found, were difficult enough in the dry weather,
but in the rainy season they would have been impossible
had it not been for the building up of the road from Narathiwat to Pattani and beyond. It was this that brought home
to Brenda the way in which events had been timed. There
had been a purpose in the disappointing delays in getting
the leprosy work started. Year after year the countryside
was flooded, and even the main highway was often under

water, so that travelling by bus was like being in a boat, with the water almost covering the wheels. Cycling was out of the question, and taxis went temporarily out of business. How could the remoter places have been reached in such circumstances? But in the very year that the clinics were open Korean engineers appeared on the scene to super-intend the raising of the highway above the flood waters, and after that travelling on it was no longer a difficulty, even if the last part of one's journey had to be by boat instead of walking across the fields to one's destination.

These journeys to individual patients were part and parcel of the leprosy nurse's task, involving considerable physical effort and endurance at times, what with wading through streams, and cycling along narrow paths between rice-fields, carrying one's bike over planks that served as bridges, all in the burning heat of a tropical sun. It was tiring, too, when one arrived, for so often there was the discouragement of a patient who had given up taking the medicine, and lapsed back into despair. But as the months passed, and they began to realise that their physical condition was improving, their welcome was heart-warming, and everything seemed worth while.

About a year after the opening of the Palas clinic a man appeared one day whose leprous condition was very marked, with elongated ears dangling almost to his shoulders. He had an old woman with him, also leprous, and a lad. They were his aunt and his cousin, he explained, and they had all come for treatment. He had come a long way, from a place called Pujud. He was a Malay, and his name was Hassan.

It was through this man that the clinic in Pujud was eventually opened. After he had come once or twice to Palas he begged Brenda to go to his home and give him his treatment there. It took him so long, so many hours to reach Palas, and the reason was that he was very rarely allowed to get on the public bus. The driver and the passengers would take one look at him and then,

'You don't get on this bus!' they would say, muttering

among themselves, 'He's got leprosy! We'll all be getting
it if he gets on here. Keep him off!'

Brenda knew this to be true. Many of the leprosy patients
had the same difficulty, and Hassan was in such a poor
condition she felt she must make the effort to go to Pujud,
even though it involved going a journey of over thirty miles.
His feet and legs were so ulcerated they required regular
dressing, and if he were to be healed the only thing would
be for her to go to him. 'There are more people with leprosy
near where I live,' he told her. 'If you come to Pujud you'll
get more patients.' So she started going once a month, and
wondered if she ought to go more frequently.

Then Dr June Morgan, the leprosy doctor in Central
Thailand, visited Saiburi, and Brenda told her about Hassan.

'Will you come with me to see him?' she asked. 'He needs
an operation on his foot, and that's a job for a doctor, not
a nurse!' Then she went on, 'There are other people over
there with leprosy. One or two of them come along when I
go to see Hassan, but he says there are more that he knows
of. I'm wondering if I ought to open a clinic there. Will you
come along and see him?'

So they went to Pujud. It was thirty miles to Pattani, then
five miles along the road to Yala they came to the place, an
unimportant village, predominantly Malay, with an Islamic
School and not much else in the way of public institutions.
One of the teachers in the school, as it happened, held strong
views about the four southern provinces that had been ceded
to Thailand, but which he affirmed really belonged to
Malaya. These convictions led him to various secret meetings with other like-minded people up in the hill country.
He was not in the least interested in people with leprosy, nor
in the westerner who evidently was, although he could not
have failed to know of her visits to the home of Hassan up
the lane off the main road. He knew what went on in Pujud,
his home town, even when he left for the hills for good. As
for Brenda, she did not even know of his existence. Her

mind was on Hassan, and what the visit of a doctor might mean to him.

The operation on his foot was performed simply and easily. No anaesthetics were necessary, for all feeling had long since left the limb. The doctor's experienced eye and skilful fingers ran over the ulcerated foot and then, hey presto, she was holding up a bone!

'The doctor, she just pulled out my toe,' exclaimed Hassan, describing the event afterwards with mingled pride and amazement. 'She just pulled it out—just like this!' and with thumb and forefinger gave a demonstration of the incredible feat.

As the doctor and the nurse, chuckling together, returned to Saiburi, the matter of opening a clinic in Pujud came up again.

'It's a long way from Saiburi, and it would mean giving up a whole day to it regularly. It's no use starting if we can't keep it up.'

'It would be worth it, though, if there really are a number of leprosy folk there. You can deal with more at one clinic than in a whole day going round the countryside.'

'We really need the Lord's guidance about this.' And as they talked, they came to the conclusion that this was one of the occasions when they could pray for a definite indication as to whether or not a clinic should be opened. They would do it in a reasonable manner. They would fix a figure.

'Lord,' they prayed. 'If it is in Your plan that a clinic should be opened at Pujud, let us meet five people with leprosy—five at least, next time we go. If five people turn up, then we'll take it it's Your will to open a clinic.'

Ten days later Brenda went again to Pujud, and got the answer to their prayer. Not merely five, but eight people with leprosy turned up at Hassan's house.

That is why a fortnightly clinic was held in Pujud until the day when Minka and Margaret were kidnapped there.

*

Although the weekly visit to Palas was like a gleaming thread in the warp and woof of Minka's life, the hospital at Saiburi was the main fabric. Here her days and nights were spent, for nurses and Thai staff all lived on the compound among the palm trees, gradually being beautified by the introduction of carefully-tended flowering shrubs. To outward appearances it was a charming spot, within easy reach of the sheltered lagoon where sandy beaches provided ideal sites for picnic breakfasts or suppers, but closer inspection into living conditions in those early days revealed limitations to comfort and convenience as irritating as an ill-fitting shoe.

The missionary nurses all lived under one roof. Each had a small bedroom, but they were only separated from each other by partitions through which every sound penetrated easily. Coughs could be heard almost from one end of the bedroom block to the other, and if you wanted to hold a private conversation the best way to do it was to stroll down the uneven path to the beach. The chances were you could find a spot there where you'd be neither interrupted nor overheard.

Meals were taken in a common dining room, where the high-spirited and garrulous provided daily opportunities for the exercise of patience, and those who preferred eating in silence were suspected of having something on their minds. Conversation tended to get sucked back to the subject they all knew they ought to avoid—the work of the hospital and the problems connected therewith. Well-intentioned and strenuous efforts to introduce other topics were liable to end, sooner or later, in a silence which was eventually broken by an observation or a complaint about something that had happened on the wards—or had *not* happened on the wards. In some ways it was a relief to get back to a subject familiar to all, and which required no mental effort in making a contribution to the conversation. But since the medical team derived from countries as far removed as Australia and England, Switzerland and North America, with differing views about how a hospital in the tropics should be run, what was the correct relationship between doctor and nurse, and whether the claims of the hospital should take priority over language study, it is perhaps not surprising that in one of her letters to her Prayer Companions Minka asked them 'especially to pray for us as missionaries. We all have our own characters. Living with many in such close quarters is not always easy. How the devil loves to get into us and let friction and irritation come between us, when with all our hearts we want to work for our Lord.'

This sense of involvement with the others went very deep in Minka. Whatever might be the tensions between them at times, she knew their basic desires were the same, and her letters were liberally sprinkled with the pronouns 'we' and 'our' as distinct from the 'I' and 'my' which characterised some. The ward services, the evangelistic campaigns conducted by the men missionaries, the progress of the little group of Christians at Saiburi market, projects in which the part she played was a minor one rather than as leader or one with a distinctive role, nevertheless loomed large in her reports home. A self-appointed commentator, she introduced her friends in New Zealand and Holland to the work of God in South Thailand.

During that first year at Saiburi Christian Hospital at River Mouth Site, an event occurred which touched the whole missionary team.

'On 15th June our eldest lady missionary, Mrs Harris, died, after being in the hospital for five days. Early on the 16th June the first missionary child was born in the hospital,' added Minka never able to hide her joy when another child was brought into the world. Then she continued:

'In the afternoon the funeral service of Mrs Harris, which was in English, Thai and Malay, was held in the hospital hall which was decorated with flowers. The burial ground is next to the hospital and the Thai officials were most helpful, allowing us to choose the plot we wanted. The plot chosen is on the border of the hospital compound.'

It was the first time any of the Malays in Saiburi had seen how the Christians bury their dead, and a large number of them had gathered to witness the interesting event. Slowly the group of missionaries moved across the compound, following the coffin, and then came the proclamation of the hope that animated them, for the predominating theme of a Christian funeral is the resurrection.

'Jesus said, I am the resurrection and the life. He that believeth in Me, though he were dead, yet shall he live . . .' The Malays looked on, surprised at the absence of any display of grief. Then they saw the old man whose wife lay in the coffin, and whom many of them knew, come forward and stand where they could hear, his face uplifted with a smile.

'Mr Harris himself, with a strong jubilant voice read in Malay "I am the way, the truth and the life," and other Scripture verses,' reported Minka, deeply moved. 'What a testimony! When the coffin was slowly let down into the grave we sang, "He lives! He lives!" Great was the number of onlookers. How each one of us is looking to the Lord of Life to give life to many of them.'

Each one of us is looking to the Lord of Life to give life . . .

They were all in it together, as Minka saw it. And not only those who were at the hospital, either. When, a few months later, she had something of special joy to report, she commenced her letter to Prayer Companions:

'To God be the glory! He has started to answer your and our prayers concerning conversions in the hospital.' This was something in which they were involved, she must let them know it. Then she went on to tell of a Chinese patient, Mr Li, suffering from incurable cancer, who understood very little of the preaching in the wards because it was in Thai, and whose condition suddenly worsened.

'He was terrified, and the Lord knew it. The afternoon before Mr Li became so very ill Mr Kuhn, one of our Mis-

sion directors, arrived in Saiburi for a short visit. This was
the Lord's answer for this needy heart. Mr Kuhn was able
to bring to this man in his own language, the glad tidings.
Mr Li read Gospel portions, but to hear someone tell and
explain made it real to him. The Lord worked in this heart,
and when he died four days later, we knew he was with the
Lord. The change in the expression on his face after he had
made his decision was remarkable.'

Minka was a team member. It might be said to be her distinctive role. 'When there is the need for a shoulder at the
wheel, Minka's shoulder is there—for just as long as it is
needed,' said one of her colleagues. The part she herself
played was scarcely worth speaking about, she felt—it was
what the team as a whole was doing that mattered. On the
occasions when she was thrust into the foreground, as during the year when she had to deputise for Juppy as the hospital evangelist to the Malays, everyone knew she was under
strain. At one conference of missionaries, when the subject
of hospital evangelism came up for discussion she burst into
tears and asked to resign. To stand up day after day and
give a talk on some aspect of the Gospel in front of a company of Malays, with missionary and Thai colleagues sometimes listening in the background, went right against the
grain of her nature. When Juppy's furlough was prolonged
'it was not easy again to shoulder the responsibility which I
had hoped so much to hand over to her,' she wrote. She
felt so much more at ease in the background.

It was different out in the little clinics for the leprosy
patients, when with unselfconscious animation she would
talk to ones and twos, or when she snatched time from midwifery to go with Brenda to some isolated shack like Jit's,
where she could minister with those hands of hers that were
so swift and gentle to cleanse and soothe. Tears sprang to
her eyes sometimes when she bent over the lad to dress his
sores, or try to ease the fever which often assailed him in
those early days when he started taking the medicine. She
tried to devise ways of occupying his time, too. He could

rarely be persuaded to emerge from his shack, and for so long had lived in isolation he spoke only when urged to make some response to a question. However, he had attended school for a few years before it was discovered he had leprosy, so he was able to read and began to study the booklets they brought for him. By the time Minka left Thailand for her second furlough, in 1967, Brenda's regular visits to care for Jit were proving effective, and he was beginning to show signs of returning to life, physically and mentally. Yet he remained withdrawn, without animation, as one who has no hope or expectation, for whom life holds nothing.

It was at this point that Margaret Morgan came on the scene. She had already been in charge of a ward in the hospital for the best part of a year, and naturally took her share in the evangelistic work connected with it. This involved visiting patients who had returned to their homes, especially those who had given evidence of faith in the Lord Jesus Christ of whom they had heard in the hospital. One of these was a woman who lived in Khuan, the same village as Jit, and after Margaret had gone to see her in her home, she was taken on to see Jit, since he lived nearby.

The subject she spoke to him about was the one on which she had prepared her first little sermon in Thai, entitled 'Are you afraid?'

A week later she went again, with Audrey Neal, an Australian who had been accompanying Brenda to preach to the Malay patients in the leprosy clinics. After the first words of greeting Jit looked at Margaret and said:

'I am afraid.' Then he continued, 'I am afraid of sin. I am afraid of the power it has over me . . .'

The two missionaries were amazed. In the first place, it was not like Jit to say so much, or to speak spontaneously like that. In the second place, they were amazed that he gave expression to fear of sin. Fear of the bandits, fear of the spirits, fear of illness, fear of death . . . these fears people were easily made conscious of, but it was not often that Margaret had heard anyone give voice to the fear that was the main point of what she had to say.

'As Audrey Neal and I listened to Jit we realised that it was evidence of the Holy Spirit working in his heart,' she wrote to her Prayer Companions. 'We had the privilege then of pointing him to the One who was able to deliver him from all fear and from the power of sin. Quite simply he received the Lord into his heart.'

'How full of praise to God we are as Jit is the "first fruits" of our leprosy work here in South Thailand!'

From that time the radical change in Jit was manifest. Physically his progress was still slow, and socially he was under the same disadvantage, for his family and neighbours continued to shun him. The only visitors to his little shack were the missionaries, and occasionally one or two Thai Christians from Saiburi. But Jit knew in a way much deeper than busy people with full lives the presence of the Lord, and as he studied the Bible which was now like a doorway into an entirely new dimension of life, the potential of his mind as well as his spirit became evident. Jit had latent talents that were unsuspected by those who had seen him for several years as a sullen, animal-like creature crouching in his hut.

'It was such a thrill to see him and hear him ask questions about the things he did not understand from his Bible,' wrote Minka on her return from furlough, adding, 'That shy but wonderful smile did something to me!'

However, that was not all she had to say in her first letter after she arrived back in Saiburi from a furlough in which she had seen every member of her beloved family, scattered now as far apart as New Zealand and Australia, Holland and Brazil. Her love for the leprosy patients, combined with the fact that most of them were Malay, the people whose language she understood well and spoke fluently, was leading the Mission leaders to the conclusion that she should be released from her full-time midwifery work in the hospital to give at least part-time help in the expanding leprosy programme. She was sent for four months to Manorom Hospital in Central Thailand for training and experience, then returned to Saiburi to live in the little house in the market which was occupied by two other missionaries whose work led them among the Malays.

As always, Minka found the change hard. For nearly ten years the Christian Hospital near the lagoon had been her home, and the busy, communal life of which she was a part the background with which she was familiar. Now she was in a small private house on the street, no longer in the same way a member of a self-contained and varied community. 'It probably does not sound right to you, but I have to admit that I am not really settled yet,' she wrote. 'To me it is very strange not to belong to the hospital any more.' It was, perhaps, the type of life to which she was best fitted socially, to which her childhood in Java had accustomed her—the large, well-kept compound with its palms and flowering shrubs, the varied community with Thai and Malay employees as well as missionaries from half-a-dozen different countries, the sense of belonging to them all, yet being dependent on none. Everyone at Saiburi knew Minka, and knew they could turn to her for help of any sort if they needed it. The petite Thai girl language teacher who stood apprehensively looking at the flood waters through which she would have to wade for nearly a mile to get from the market to Saiburi Hospital gasped with relief when she saw a tall figure coming towards her and recognised Minka.

'Oh, Minka, are you going to the hospital? May I come with you?' she asked, and Minka responded with her ready smile, 'Yes, of course. Come along!' and held out her hand. Together they waded through the water that got higher and higher, until the Thai girl, half laughing, half frightened, grasped Minka's arm with both of her little hands, clinging to her until they reached the compound. 'I can remember to this day the feeling of security as I walked through the flood water with Minka,' she wrote years later. There was something symbolic to her about that journey, and she could almost hear Minka saying, 'Gaysinee, you mustn't be frightened about the future. God is holding on to you, just as I did.'

When a Pakistani man from Saiburi died suddenly on the pilgrimage to Mecca one year, it was to Minka the family turned, asking her to break the news to his eldest daughter. 'Her love and sympathy helped to soften the blow, as the injection she thoughtfully took along with her helped to overcome the physical effects of the shock.' It was typical of Minka that she took along an injection. She never got flustered in an emergency, as Russell Gray, a fellow missionary, had occasion to be thankful for when he fell through the roof where he was doing a repairing job, and landed on the cement floor with such velocity that he broke the cement. 'I thought I had had it! But Minka was in in a moment and had me stretched out on a flat hard door on the floor, and there she made me lie for three to four days. She got all the necessary things to keep me in that position and under her care I recovered and have felt no ill effects from it since. My wife was very grateful!'

Margaret Morgan, who by this time was well established on the nursing staff at Saiburi, had developed along quite different lines. Under the gentle exterior there was a very definite, determined little person, as everyone knew, with a way of planning everything meticulously and thoroughly. But the unexpected was likely to throw her off balance. She told the story against herself when she related to a friend how she had been on an air flight with a fellow missionary known to be a diabetic, and who suddenly started laughing and pointing unreasonably. So far from recognising the symptoms, Margaret, who was feeling rather air-sick, tried to see the joke. And when, eventually, it dawned on her what was happening, and she quickly called the stewardess to bring some food, for all that she was an experienced and well-trained nurse, she started trying to feed the invalid with egg rather than with sugar!

Where Minka was strictly impartial in her attitude to others, Margaret took a special interest in individuals and would sometimes spend hours talking to one or another whom she felt to be in spiritual difficulty. Perhaps it was this cultivation of friendship with particular people that led her again to the village of Khuan, where Jit lived, to follow up a woman patient she had helped to nurse in hospital, Mrs Jong, and a man named Mr Jai.

'I want to mention to you again the village of Khuan,' she wrote during the last year before she was due to return to England on furlough. 'You will remember that I told you of three who have professed to believe there, Jit, Mrs Jong and Mr Jai. Jit is quite apart from the others because of his leprosy. When I wrote to you in May, Jit had only recently put his trust in the Lord. Now he is cause for real praise as he is growing in the Lord and reading his New Testament every day . . .

'Recently I have been appointed co-ordinator of the work at Khuan.' Not much more could be done than to arrange a programme in which some of the missionaries on the hospital staff went there periodically, but Margaret made the plan very carefully. 'At present there is little to see, but who knows what the Lord will do as you pray? Many folk from the village have been to the hospital and I feel that there are others who are really interested in spiritual things . . .

'Planning visits is not easy because of duties here at the hospital,' she continued. There were other reasons why it was not easy either, notably the fact that she was battling against recurring attacks of dysentery, and trying to learn Malay and Thai at the same time. 'We are managing one or two a month at present.' But a few months later she reported having been there with another missionary, to stay for a week.

'The Lord certainly blessed in answer to your prayers. We returned yesterday tired but most encouraged at the response from the people . . . children came in before and after school, and two Thai girls in their teens slept with us at night, also various folk kept coming to visit us, so we were rarely alone. We also had the rats and chickens for company! We bathed Thai style at the well morning and evening, dressed in a wide tubular cloth hitched under the arms. One is constantly fearful that it will slip down, but we got quite expert eventually! We ate Thai food cooked very nicely by my friend, Mrs Jong.'

There was an unexpected outcome from that week in Khuan, with daily visiting in the mornings and afternoons, children's meetings in the evenings followed by what had been planned to be a short Bible study and time of prayer for the handful of believers. '. . . but from the first night others joined in, until on Sunday night we had eight men and two women present. For Thailand this is most encouraging. We rarely get eight Thai men together at the same time even here in Saiburi.' Twenty teenagers and adults enrolled for a Bible Correspondence Course. Seven or eight of the men expressed an earnest desire to learn more about the Christian faith that had been lived out and proclaimed before them, and Mr Jai started talking about renting a shop that could be used for trading during the day, and meetings in the evenings.

Shortly after that visit Margaret returned to England, having written ahead to the Home Director there that during her furlough she would like to get some instruction in the disease of leprosy. And in the report filed at Singapore it was recorded that 'Margaret has done an outstanding job as a first termer. She has led souls to the Lord, her general influence has been good.' Then there was added the prophetic note,

'Her burden for leprosy work will lead her to clinics rather than to hospital . . .'

CHAPTER SIX

SHADOWS IN THE SUNLIGHT

From Margaret Morgan's notebook

My child I know
Take comfort from the fact that I know
What is weighing on your heart
I know your circumstances
I know and I care and I love you.
Trust Me to lighten your load
Trust Me to bear it with you
Allow Me to share it
My child, look up to Me
Look up and rejoice—be glad—sing
praises to Me and let Me turn
your sadness to joy
your spirit of heaviness to a spirit of praise and thanksgiving
Do not bear the burden alone
this is not My way.
Share with Me
Share with others
'Rejoice always
Pray constantly
Give thanks in all circumstances
for this is the will of God in Christ Jesus for YOU.'

M.M.

When concerned for a friend needing an operation

THE WASHING OF feet was part of the leprosy nurse's job. Brenda, Minka, whoever happened to be the nurse at the clinic, knew it had to be done. The feet weren't just dirty feet, either. They could be very unpleasant feet indeed, with dead flesh and ulcers oozing pus, and emitting a stench that made you catch your breath and want to get away in case you started to retch. As a leprosy nurse, of course, you did neither, although you knew that however carefully you washed those feet and cleaned those sores, it would do nothing to arrest the disease, which only the right drugs taken at the right times in the correct doses could heal. The disease was out of sight, a condition of the nerves, and no amount of washing of the skin or mollifying of the sores with ointment could affect it. But if you didn't get those wounds cleansed and closed your patient could die of the infection before he died of the leprosy. And since you wanted him to live, you dealt with those wounds that were mainly due to carelessness. If people put their hands on burning embers, or walked on thorns and broken glass, of course their skin would be pierced! The problem with leprosy was that it left the affected parts insensitive, so that cuts did not hurt and burns gave no pain, and the damage was done without being realised.

'I don't know why my foot has got like this—I didn't feel anything,' the patients who came limping to the clinic would say, as likely as not adding with a fatalism born of Islam,

'It's the will of Allah!' You saw the rotting limb and the filthy flesh and knew you could not leave that fellow human being in his careless misery, so you washed the limb and bound it up with clean rags, and gave it a pat and the patient a smile and said, 'Now keep it covered up and don't let any dirt get into it, and we'll see if it's better next time I come!'

It had happened scores, hundreds of times, this washing of feet, and there was probably nothing different about the occasion in the Pujud clinic when Minka washed Uncle Mat's foot, then took it on her lap to cut away the dead skin and clean it up. The preliminary routine had been just as usual, with Brenda's quick eyes taking in the grouping of patients to see which would be the best spot to leave clear for Anne before setting out her medicines and bandages. Anne Wilding's job was to talk to the patients, explain the Bible pictures, and proclaim in as relevant a way as possible the everlasting Gospel. The leprosy team regarded this proclamation as the most important part of the whole procedure, and on occasion when the missionaries were all in conclave, formulating policies, raised their voices with clear insistence that a Malay-speaking evangelist should always be at a clinic. A nurse could not do the two jobs single-handed. It happened sometimes that the nurse had to try, since no-one was free to go with her, but usually there were two in the team at each clinic, and on the particular occasion when Minka tackled Uncle Mat she was acting as nurse, while one of the others did the preaching.

Uncle Mat was a redoubtable character. He came originally from Kelantan in Malaya, and why and when he decided to put the border between him and his native land and settle in Thailand was not a matter to ask questions about. What was known was that he had had seven or eight wives in his time and got rid of them all through his temper. He did not deny that before contracting leprosy he had been connected with a gang of terrorists, and had seen the inside of a gaol for quite a long period on that account. It was also rumoured that he had deliberately committed a murder when his blood was up. He didn't deny that, either.

He was a pitiable-enough object when he limped into the Pujud clinic with his body weakened and his fortunes low, but adversity had done little to subdue his angry spirit. He had come with no desire at all to hear what the people who ran the clinic had to tell him about their Christ. As a Muslim he wanted none of that, although what he had read in a little tract he had received some years previously had made him decide he would go along to the leprosy clinic to see if these Christians could do anything to put him on his feet. He had been surprised and impressed by Brenda's open friendliness, Anne's patience in answering his questions, the general care in treating him. His innate arrogance had not been provoked, and he was in a quiet frame of mind when Minka sat on the little low stool the nurses used for the foot-cleaning process, and took his foot on her lap to treat the ulcer.

Something happened to Uncle Mat in that moment. The simple, unselfconscious action was one he had seen many times in the clinic, so it was not new to him, but on this occasion it had a divine quality about it, and he was touched as he had never been touched before in his life.

'. . . the humility and love she showed overwhelmed me,' he said years later, 'I know now that what I felt was Christ reaching out to me through her. Though I hadn't understood anything about the Gospel, yet in that moment my resistance to the Lord crumbled. That is when I started on the path of faith . . .'

But the team in the clinic knew nothing about it that day, nor for a long time after, and as far as they could see they were making no headway at all, spiritually, where the Malays were concerned. It was the same story in the hospital, and in Yala and Pattani and Narathiwat, and over on the other side of the peninsula in Satun. There were Thai who had responded to the proclamation of the news about Jesus, and Chinese too, though they comprised only a small percentage of the population. There had been a number of baptisms,

Sunday services were being held regularly in several centres, dramatic changes in the lives of some of the new believers gave clear evidence of the new life imparted to them by the Holy Spirit. But among them was not one Malay.

Not one Malay. After more than a decade of visitation to kampongs, discussions in Islamic schools, specially-organised campaigns when the best Malay speakers among the missionaries delivered carefully-prepared talks, showed film strips, drew lightning sketches and prayed with all the earnestness of which they were capable that God would break through and save souls, nothing seemed to have happened. Hundreds gathered, showed a measure of interest and occasionally a hotly-argumentative spirit, took tracts, and dispersed. Hopes had been raised high on two or three occasions when here and there a Muslim had professed faith in Christ, but no lasting result was to be seen. And now things seemed at their lowest ebb for years. For one reason or another all the men missionaries who could speak Malay had left South Thailand, and the only opportunity the handful of women who knew the language had of conversing with Malay men was when they came for treatment to the hospital or the leprosy clinics. Evangelism among them was virtually at a standstill.

The hospital was labouring under difficulties too, especially on the nursing side which was seriously under-staffed. In addition to normal ward duties the missionary nurses had the supervising and training of about forty young Thai girls whose language they understood but imperfectly. The task of language-learning seemed never-ending. 'I never get any time to study' was the valid reason, not the excuse, for failure to achieve fluency. At one stage Brenda and Minka had to accept the ultimatum that the leprosy work could be extended no further at present, since the nurses who had been working on shifts of twelve to fourteen hours for about three months were in danger of breaking down. 'Between the two of us we give ten days a month to work in the wards,' wrote Minka, who observed humorously on another occasion that four days a week on the wards and the remaining three on leprosy work left her with no reason for being bored. 'Being so short-staffed, of course, also means that the new block for leprosy patients cannot be opened yet.'

Money to build the isolation block for the leprosy work had been provided in full, and the building was completed. Embarrassing questions were sometimes asked as to why it wasn't being used yet, and the answer was always the same — lack of staff. But until that ward was opened no leprosy patients could be admitted to the hospital, no matter how serious their condition. The widespread and deep-seated fear of the disease was so great that other patients would have revolted and most of the Thai staff gone on strike. The doctors knew their well-founded argument that leprosy was not nearly as infectious or dangerous as some of the diseases no-one seemed to worry about made no difference to the general attitude. Leprosy was to be dreaded, and those suffering from it shunned. Anyone bearing the tell-tale stigma of elongated ears, flattened noses, maimed fingers or stumps instead of feet was likely to be an outcast for life, however convincing the evidence the foreign doctors produced that complete healing had been effected.

Jit came into this category. The new drugs administered so regularly and carefully over several years had had their effect. Recent tests had proved negative. Jit was clear of the disease, and there was no doubt but that he was non-infectious. The doctors asserted it. The nurses asserted it. A written testimonial to that effect asserted it. But the people of Khuan remained unconvinced. Jit had lived in the little lean-to beside his home for years, and his own family still avoided him. His daily ration of rice was brought to him and deposited by someone who kept at a safe distance and hurried away when the duty was performed. Of course he had leprosy! Look at his twisted face and stumps of fingers! Keep away from him!

By this time a missionary couple, Alan and Maelynn Ellard, were living in the village, and their two little girls,

Brenda and Alison, were known to be the joy of Minka's heart. The twin toddlers were brought along to the leprosy clinic at Palas nearly every Wednesday to see Auntie Minka, and her face would light up at the sight of them. 'Oh, you darlings!' she would say, 'I'd love to come and give you a hug! But I can't—I'm too dirty. (Don't let them come to this end, Maelynn—keep them up there, away from any chance of infection. It's lovely for me just to look at them!) When I come to stay with you for the weekend, all fresh and clean, then I'll be able to hug you, won't I? And I've got something special for you to play with. You'll see!'

On the occasions when she spent a day or two with the family that had become very dear to her everybody noticed the care she took of the two little girls, and the time she spent with them, and the way their parents left them in her charge. 'They're my grandchildren!' she would say laughingly, and people would nod and say to each other, 'She loves them just as though she really is their grandmother.'

The knowledge that people were talking like this gave Minka an idea. The Ellards were preparing to return to Britain on furlough, and she had gone to help them with their packing. She had a suggestion to make to Maelynn, though, that had nothing to do with the matter on hand. It had to do with Jit.

'Shall I take Brenda and Alison out for a walk?' she asked. 'I could take them to see Jit. That ought to prove to everyone that he's free from infection.'

'What a good idea!' replied Maelynn. 'You do that, and I'll get on with the packing.' So off they set, the tall white-haired woman and the two chubby little fair-haired children with her. Along the village street they went, and the people who saw them called out in friendly greeting,

'Where are you going?'

'Oh, we're going to see Jit,' said Minka, smiling and walking slowly on.

'To see Jit!' Smiles gave place to expressions of surprise and alarm. 'Taking the children to Jit!'

'Oh, yes, Jit's not infectious now, you know. It's quite safe to take the children. He'll be so pleased to see them!'

'She's taking the children to see Jit!' they murmured, incredulously looking at each other in amazement. 'It must be true then,' they added. 'He must be all right. She'd never take the children to his hut if there was any danger. Jit must be all right.'

That simple action accomplished more than all the words of doctors and nurses and the official pieces of paper that could be produced to re-establish Jit as a member of the community, for the word got around. Minka had taken the missionary's two little girls, in broad daylight, to see Jit in his hut! He had been seen to talk to them, and they had touched him! Their mother knew all about it, too, and didn't mind a bit! They'd been saying Jit wasn't infectious any more, but this proved it.

From that time the attitude of the villagers towards him began to change, and his own fear of being chased off subsided. Perhaps one of the biggest milestones of his life was passed when, a few weeks later, he walked out of Khuan with Margaret Morgan to attend a one-day convention organised for Thai Christians with leprosy held at Saiburi hospital. Minka, who had been elsewhere to collect other patients for the event, wrote:

'As soon as we got to Khuan I strained my eyes to see the first glimpse of Jit. I am afraid I cannot describe what went through me when I saw him standing there. That big smile! Oh! What a wonderful God we have who gave this young man, after being "imprisoned" for nearly thirteen years, the courage to leave his hut and come out!'

There were others at the convention whose lot was similar to that of Jit, as Minka reported in her crisp, vivid manner. 'It is wonderful to find how much the Holy Spirit has been teaching this despised and lonely man in his little hut in a huge plantation,' she wrote of one patient who travelled seventy-two miles to come. And of another,

'Mr Juan told us that the Lord had a number of times

preserved his life when he wanted to commit suicide; how he went to a leprosarium in the north where he found the Saviour. When he was declared healed he had come back to his home near Khuan, but was despised by everyone because he is rather deformed. And so he prayed that he might be "found" by a Christian. He had to wait to have that prayer answered for two years, but last year Alan Ellard "found" him.'

The parables of the Good Shepherd became touchingly and poignantly relevant at that first convention for the Christian leprosy patients—and also the lines of the little chorus some of the missionaries had sung back in the home-lands they had left:

> Mine are the hands to do the work,
>   My feet shall run for Thee,
> My lips shall sound the glorious news,
>   Lord, here am I, send me.

Meanwhile Margaret's expectation of doing leprosy work had been only partially fulfilled. On her return from furlough she had been sent to Manorom for a month's training and experience in treating the disease, but she knew her main work would continue to be in the general wards of Saiburi Hospital for the best part of a year, to take the place of one of the nurses who was going on furlough. As things turned out she remained there for over two years, supervising the pharmacy and acting as midwife, for the nurse whose place she was taking did not return. The only opportunity she had of putting into practice what she had learned about the treatment of leprosy patients at Manorom was during a month when she helped in the weekly clinic at Saiburi.

However, she had experienced something at Manorom during that month in 1969 which made it always memorable to her, though she spoke of it only to one or two of her closest friends. She had gone there conscious of a deep spiritual hunger. Her first term of service on the mission field, followed by her first furlough at home, were behind her now. All illusions had been shorn from the task to which she had been called, and the excitement of returning home with all that was involved in travelling and speaking at meetings had left her exhausted. She was entering on the second stage of her missionary career feeling unready for the demands it would make. Four weeks in one of the nurses' homes in the hospital at Manorom, where she would have no responsibilities outside the course of practical training in leprosy, would provide her with just what she needed and longed for—more time to spend quietly in her room, waiting on God. She spent hours studying the epistles of Paul, particularly to find what was revealed about the Holy Spirit's energising power in the life of the believer.

It was no new subject to her. 'I can remember in the early days of our friendship that she had a great hunger for the Lord,' wrote one of her closest friends. 'A church near Mount Hermon was having teaching on revival and the ministry of the Holy Spirit, and Margaret was very interested in this. Before she went out she did have a fresh encounter with the Lord, and remembered testifying to having been filled with the Holy Spirit, but later on she wondered if she was right to have done so.'

Perhaps it was the memory of her own doubts about speaking too freely of inner experiences which made her more reticent to tell others of the sense of inner release she first began to enjoy during that month at Manorom. Prayer which could be expressed without the mental exercise of finding words enriched her times of private worship, and there was a perceptible increase of spiritual power in her life.

She left Manorom 'bubbling over with anticipation of what the Lord was going to do' as her friends there noticed when she set out again for Saiburi, but before she even reached it she had an encounter in Yala which proved to be by divine appointment. The missionaries in South Thailand had given out thousands of tracts in an effort to reach as many people as possible, and one of these had fallen into the hands of a woman named Mrs Deng. It brought her, eagerly wanting to know more, to the address given on the tract just about the time Margaret arrived there on her way to Saiburi. The outcome of the talk they had together was that Mrs Deng's heart, like Lydia's of old, was opened by the Lord, and she left the house fully assured of her salvation. Six months later Margaret, who kept in touch with her, was writing to her prayer companions that Mrs Deng had already led four others to Christ, and with tears running down her face had expressed her ardent longing to serve Him with all her time and strength.

As for Margaret herself, the headaches and bouts of sickness persisted as usual, and there were times when she 'had a good cry and felt better for it'. But it was noticeable that she spoke much more freely to patients about God's way of salvation, and when she led a meeting, either in Thai or in English, there was something exceptionally enlivening about it. She was not an orator, the part she played in the evangelistic and pastoral work of the South Thailand team was comparatively small, but it was observed that what she did, she did well.

'She is very faithful, has a love for souls, and keen spiritual insight,' wrote the Field Superintendent in a private report to the Directors in Singapore, adding that she accepted without complaint the work she had been given to do though it was not what she would have chosen. This had been evident when she was asked to continue in the hospital work and relinquish for another year the plan to become a full-time leprosy nurse. And although the hospital's need was obvious, and Margaret recognised it, making no demur at the delay, the Superintendent himself was uneasy about it. He felt an important principle was in danger of being violated. In a Mission that required of each of its members the assurance of divine guidance in life and service, it was contravening its own code to ignore or crush convictions. As was clearly outlined in the *Principles and Practice* which she had signed, workers would not be appointed to a permanent sphere of work without their full concurrence, though all were 'expected to be willing to render temporary help when this was deemed necessary'.

At what point did temporary pass into the category of permanent?

'Margaret has wanted to get into the leprosy programme since the term before this one,' he pointed out. 'When it seems that something might be done about it something else turns up that apparently makes it necessary for Margaret to keep on in the hospital. So besides this not being right, there might come a time when she is no more willing to continue in the hospital work.'

The reason for this observation was the proposed return of Margaret to England on a short early furlough in order that she would be back in time to relieve a nurse shortage in Saiburi Hospital later on. It suited her personal desires very well, for her sister Elaine was preparing to be married and the warm-hearted congregation at the Tabernacle in Porth had already subscribed nearly enough to provide Margaret with a two-way air ticket so that she could be present at the wedding. To prolong her stay in England for a few months in order that she could remain longer in Thailand on her return seemed reasonable enough. What should then be the permanent nature of her work, however, was not so clear. Would it continue to be confined to the hospital, or would it be among sufferers from leprosy?

She had been home for about three months when a clear indication of what the future held for her came through something quite unexpected that happened in America. Brenda Holton's colleague, the leprosy nurse who was on furlough there, resigned from the Mission because she felt God was calling her to work among the Thai in Chicago. Someone must be prepared to step in when the time came

for Minka and then for Brenda to go on furlough. At least
two full-time leprosy nurses were needed to run the clinics
and visit patients in outlying districts.

Margaret knew intuitively what it would mean for her
when she heard the news. Leprosy nursing was of such a
character that it required not only a specialised training but
a sense of vocation. A volunteer, not a recruit, was needed
to fill the place left empty, and Margaret had already expressed her desire to work among the leprosy patients. She
was the obvious one to be drafted into the leprosy team, and
it was arranged that on her return to Thailand she would
first go to Manorom for three months' training and experience before going back to Saiburi. Then she would be
equipped when the time came to step into the gap.

On the face of it, the pending appointment might have
been expected to bring joy and happy anticipation to Margaret as she saw in view at last the fulfilment of her early
conviction that she would one day work in the rural clinics
for leprosy patients. In a way, it did so. But time, that great
tester of purposes, had stripped any glamour from the pro-
ject. She knew from personal experience how distasteful
the work could be, the dreariness of the surroundings, the
discouraging reaction of patients. She knew how quickly she
got a headache when walking in the sun, and that visits to
patients in remote villages inevitably entailed walking in the
sun. She knew the effect travelling on the buses so often
had on her too—those overcrowded buses with their cargo
of humans and livestock and vegetables and strongly smell-
ing fish. The journeys could leave her drained of energy,
and afraid that her 'tummy would play up again'. It was bad
enough on duty in hospital when she felt ill and had to
remain on the wards because there was no-one to relieve
her, but it would be worse to feel ill in a leprosy clinic at
the end of a thirty-mile journey with no transport but the
public bus to get her back home.

She tried to make light of it in the living room in Taff
Street when she was talking it over with Mum, but Mum

was against the whole idea, and said so. 'You can't stand that sort of life, Margaret,' she protested. 'It will be too much for you . . .

'Well, if you feel you must, I suppose you must, but I want you to promise me something. Promise you won't drive yourself and get so ill you can't be brought back home here, where I can look after you!'

She felt uneasy. She remembered a remark Margaret had made six or seven years before, when she was setting out for the East for the first time. 'I'm not going to have a long life, you know, Mum.' Margaret had said it quite casually, and probably forgotten all about it, but Mrs Morgan hadn't. 'I'm not going to have a long life . . .' Why had she said that? What did it mean?

Alma Taylor was uneasy, too, though for a different reason. She broached the subject rather cautiously, when she and Margaret were on one of the walks on the hills above Porth which they took together when Margaret was not away somewhere, speaking at meetings.

'What about the bandits?' she asked. 'Tell me about them, Margaret.'

Margaret didn't answer immediately. It was a matter of policy with the South Thailand team not to talk about the complex problems of the border country. Undoubtedly there were bandits, she admitted. There had been unrest ever since she first arrived in South Thailand, and the position hadn't improved. Sometimes people were brought into the hospital with gunshot wounds. Quite often, in fact. From time to time there were hold-ups on country roads. People kidnapped. It was fairly safe in the towns and bigger villages. There was more danger in the rural areas, especially in the hill country where the jungle lay.

The rural areas. Alma's breath came more quickly, and looking across the valley to the hills beyond she asked deliberately,

'Could you run into them if you do that leprosy work, Margaret?'

Margaret's finger went up to her lips in a way she had when she was thinking and she answered rather slowly.

'Yes, I could. I suppose it might well happen . . .'

'But Margaret . . .' Alma tried to speak without showing agitation, quietly, reasonably, 'Do you think you ought to go and take such risks? Is it right?'

'The Lord has called me,' was the steady answer, and there was nothing more to say.

Alma and Bert talked a lot to each other about her during those last months she was at home. They noticed an increasing sweetness in her character which touched them.

'Never an unkind word to say about anyone,' said Bert, reporting on the times in the little vestry at the Tabernacle when Margaret slipped in, smiling, for a chat and prayer at the beginning of the day. 'Sometimes I'll blow off about something and she'll say "Oh, don't say that, Bert! The Lord can change it, if we ask Him!" And when she's had a long, tedious journey with only a handful of people at the end of it, there's always something about the meeting that she's rejoicing over—some old lady who really loves the Lord, or a couple who were tremendously eager to pray for the Malays, or something. Never a complaint. She really is a saint, that girl!'

So the short furlough passed, and as the time drew nearer to leave home again Margaret realised the thought of the separation had never been so hard. It came to the surface of her mind unbidden one day when she was sun-bathing after a picnic in the Lake District. Her friend, with whom she was sharing the few days holiday, suddenly became aware that Margaret was quietly crying beside her.

'Margaret—what's the matter?' she asked gently. Margaret admitted it was the prospect of leaving Mum, and the indefinable fear of going back to Thailand.

Four weeks later she was back there, and in the same month the long-awaited opening of the leprosy wing took place at Saiburi Hospital, with the admission of two Malay men and more to follow. It was an event which was to prove a turning point in the work among the Muslims, though no-one could foresee it at the time.

The following month, during the dreaded fast of Ramadan, the hospital was thrown into a state of alarm when shots were fired without warning into the compound one night. There were no injuries, though there were some narrow escapes, and at least a dozen Thai nurse-aides left as a result, leaving the place seriously under-staffed, and the missionary body acutely conscious of hostile forces at work. Some felt the time had come to close the hospital. Its situation, a mile from the town and close to the lonely lagoon, made it too vulnerable. Patients would be afraid to come, and parents would be unwilling to let their girls live in as nurses aides! For a time it looked as though the prophets of doom were right, as the intake of patients fell off, and the Thai staff wanted to leave. However, a show of strength was provided by the local authorities who posted armed policemen to guard the gates, and things settled down again after a time. But a new tension had entered the situation.

A few months after this Minka left for what proved to be her last furlough. Again it took her round the world as she visited all the members of her widely-scattered family. In Holland it brought her in touch with new supporters of the work she represented, to her great delight. A church on the little island of Marhen, where tourists flock to see the people in ancient national costumes, took her to its heart. And after she had visited one large church, 'Just imagine!' she wrote to a friend, 'I preached from the same pulpit as Corrie ten Boom!'

Her journeys always brought her back to New Zealand, to Alice's home in Wellington with its blustery south winds, and to Auckland where Ringetote stood sentinel over the busy waterways leading to the harbour and golden beaches stretched lazily under blue skies. What meant more to her than the freshness and the beauty of the country in the New World that had become her own were the friends who loved her, the church that supported her, and the Bible College whose students arrived one day, en masse, to surprise her with their greetings.

'Oh!' she exclaimed incredulously as she saw them standing, row upon row of smiling young people at the door of her friend's house. It was something she never looked for or expected, any ceremony or public acclamation in honour of Minka! On one occasion, when she opened a letter addressed to her in the presence of others, they were touched at her reaction to the gift of £100 which it contained. 'Oh, no, no!' she gasped, almost in dismay. 'Not for *me*! I couldn't take it ... No, no, not for me. I shall pass it on to the Mission!' Some of her colleagues learned that the only way to give her anything without having it returned with interest was to do it anonymously—preferably with a text which implied the gift was from her Heavenly Father who was never short of cash and expected His gifts to be accepted.

It was while she was travelling by train in New Zealand that she received news from Thailand which drew from her the loud exclamation 'Praise the Lord!' Her fellow passengers looked up in surprise at the handsome, white-haired woman so eagerly devouring the contents of a letter she had just opened. The news it contained was of what had been happening in the leprosy wing at Saiburi. The translation of Luke's Gospel into their own familiar dialect by Anne Wilding, followed by discussions on it by Audrey Neal evening by evening, had had their effect on the Malay men who were living there, Uncle Mat amongst them. He was one of the first to come to faith in Christ as the Son of the living God. He was asking for baptism, and at least four others besides! The break through to the Muslims had been achieved at last, not through learned discussions in Islamic schools, not through well-planned evangelistic campaigns, but among the most despised and shunned members of the community, the sufferers from leprosy, who had been received into the only hospital open to them, the Christian Hospital at Saiburi.

Minka could not contain her joy when she read of it.

As the busy months of furlough with its full programme of meetings wore on, however, it was evident that she was not well. Her back was giving her much pain and she had lost weight. When she came back to Wellington, with only a few weeks to go before she was due to return to Thailand, she looked so ill her family was alarmed.

'Minka, you're not fit to go back!' Alice protested. And when Minka admitted that she did not want to, that this time she felt strangely reluctant to return, her family urged her not to go. 'You've done your duty for years,' they said. 'Why don't you give up missionary work now, and settle here at home?'

'I couldn't do it,' replied Minka, and they were not surprised at her response. 'I wouldn't have a moment's peace if I did.' It was what they expected, but they said to each other they were worried about her.

Minka herself was ashamed of her own lack of desire to return, and at the farewell dinner given by the Wellington Reformed Church in her honour sat listening with increasing discomfort to the speeches that were made. 'Eager to be off, back to the work she loves . . .' was the note struck, and she knew she must give the lie to it. When the moment came for her to respond she rose to her feet, a striking figure in her simple blue and white suit, and after thanking them all she went on,

'I don't want you to have false ideas about me. I don't want to go back at all. I'd rather not go. Don't think me a saint—I'm not. I'm not going back because I want to go, but because I know the Lord is sending me . . .'

So she went back. They pleaded with her to prolong her furlough until she was stronger, but there were two reasons why she knew she could not do so. One was that unless she got back to Thailand within the specified time she would forfeit her visa, and application for it would have to be started all over again. The other was that Brenda Holton's furlough was overdue, and although she realised that she might have to undergo a major operation when she reached England she was delaying going because she did not want to leave Margaret alone. Anne Wilding, whose fluent Malay and patience in talking to people while the nurse attended to patients halved the burden of the work in the leprosy clinics, was in England for family reasons, and without either nurse or evangelist to help her Margaret's strength would fail under the strain. Minka *must* go back.

Two weeks with her brother Gerald and his family in Canberra helped to restore her in measure, but it was with very mixed feelings she eventually boarded the train in Singapore which would carry her for a day and a night through Malaysia to the Thai border. 'Brenda Holton has already left for furlough and I will be living with Margaret Morgan from Wales,' she wrote to her prayer companions as she looked forward to the full programme ahead. 'With more than 300 patients on the register, I do not think that we will have to start looking for work!

'Most of you know that the Lord has given us the joy of seeing eight Muslim leprosy patients come to a real faith in Him. Pray with us that whole groups of families may come to Him so then they will be able to stand against the strong opposition and persecution they will inevitably meet with. Also at least five Thai patients have become Christians.'

Then she continued on a deeper and more personal level.

'Terrorism has flared up again and we would very much value prayer for safety, too. A new term always means facing new adjustments, but that is why the Lord gave His promi   in Matthew 28:20b. "I am with you always, even unto the end of the world." '

As she travelled alone through the rice fields and planta-tions and thick green jungles of Malaysia, she tried to stay her mind on the promise of His presence, but she did not find it easy. Her back was paining her badly, and she felt depressed. When the train pulled up at the border, and she looked out to see if there were any porters to help her with her luggage, and there were none, she thought she would have given up and gone back, if that had been possible. But it was not possible. She dragged herself out of her seat and started pulling at her cases.

It was then that the miracle happened. Quietly, inexplicably, she became aware of strength being poured into her. She lifted the cases onto the platform, and for the first time was not conscious of her back. God had met her, touched her, renewed her for the task ahead at the moment of her deepest need.

Minka straightened herself, picked up her cases, and passed painlessly over the border.

CHAPTER SEVEN

MOMENT IN PUJUD

From Margaret Morgan's notebook

My child, take great care
that nothing keep you
from the one thing that is needful.
Remember Mary
She chose to sit at my feet
To listen to what I had to say
To learn from Me.
Nothing deflected her from this
Not the disapproval of another
Nor the pressure of work to be done.
She knew what should have priority
She knew what was most needful.
My child take great care
Do not be like Martha
Distracted by much serving
Cut off from Me
by activity.
Loving Me, yes,
But seeking to communicate that love
in a wrong way.
My child, come
and sit at My feet,
be still and listen to My voice,
Then afterwards serve
As I direct
as I desire.

M.M.

Written the month before the kidnapping

PUJUD CLINIC WAS not what it used to be. Minka noticed the change as soon as she visited it after her return from furlough. In the past there had been quite a genial, club-like atmosphere about the place, with a nucleus of Malay men prepared to sit around and listen to Gospel talks on the cassettes or to chat and ask questions in a friendly way. Uncle Mat was not the only one among the first group of Malays to be baptised who had been a patient in the Pujud clinic. But they had all moved away now. Uncle Mat was in Saiburi, in charge of a ramshackle house with a piece of land where chickens pecked a living, known as the Malay Centre. Malay patients well enough to leave the leprosy wing of the hospital were finding it a good place to get rehabilitated to normal life again, and even Malays free from leprosy were getting into the habit of dropping in to listen to the cassettes, to sit around when one of the missionaries came to read parts of the Bible aloud in their own local Malay dialect, or to talk about Jesus.

At Pujud, however, it was quite different. Hassan, beside whose home the clinic was situated, remained friendly and always ready to lend a helping hand, but he adhered to his Muslim faith, doing little to quieten sneers or angry arguments against what was preached.

'For the evangelist, Anne Wilding, it really is hard going,' wrote Minka. And on the occasions when Anne was not there, it was hard going for Minka.

If Pujud clinic was a gloomy place to go to now, Palas was quite the reverse. It seemed as though scarcely a month passed without some joyful event connected with it—thirty people present at a Sunday morning service, the baptism of a Thai leprosy patient one week, and the baptism of two Malays the next, the Christmas party when deep floods failed to prevent a number turning up to celebrate for the first time the birth of the Son of Man in Bethlehem. Brenda, still in England and with an adverse medical report threatening to prevent her return to Thailand, was kept well informed of what was going on, and of the developments taking place in the leprosy work.

Minka and Margaret were living together now in a little house in Pattani, which lay conveniently situated between the two clinics. For Margaret particularly it was a new and delightful experience to have a home of her own after living for so long in the institutional atmosphere of the hospital compound. All her natural home-making instincts were aroused and found full expression in the choice of gaily-coloured curtains and cushions, pictures on the wall, and a turquoise decor for the kitchen. Instead of having her meals in a communal dining room she could sit down to a tastefully-laid table where such china as she possessed could be shown off to advantage. The early morning tea set with forget-me-not pattern given her by the girls at the Tabernacle in Porth was just right for two!

And the garden! It was the first time in her life she had had a garden, for the home in Taff Street possessed only a paved back yard. She never got over the surprise and excitement of seeing something she herself had planted growing up and bursting into flower. And since Minka had no strong preferences where household arrangements were concerned, providing they were simple, she was quite content to let Margaret plan things as she pleased.

Although the two had worked together in the hospital as colleagues for years, they had not been intimate friends, and Margaret, always very sensitive to the reactions of others, wondered how they would adjust to these new and closer circumstances. It was the sort of thing she often prayed about, this matter of relationships. 'I don't get depressed often but other emotions, reactions to people, are often aggravated by tiredness,' she confided to Mum once, in a letter home. With Minka she soon found that below superficial differences there were deeper levels on which they were at one. Both of them were quiet people, not eager to take the lead, for although Margaret was a good administrator responsibility weighed heavily on her. Each of them, at one stage in her life, had had the natural hope of marriage and motherhood and known the inner grief of disappointment, which had done its refining work before it passed away. Margaret had a simple exercise book into which she pasted neatly typed extracts of poems and sayings that had inspired her, and one of them was.

> Our loss is truest gain
> If day by day
> Christ takes the place
> Of all He takes away.

It summed up the attitude of both of them towards desires that had been relinquished. They had had a similar enrichment of their devotional lives, too, in recent years, an inner release of spirit in prayer about which they rarely spoke but which bound them together in unspoken understanding. They both enjoyed singing, particularly words of Scripture that had been set to music, and sometimes, as they prepared meals and set the table would sing quietly together. 'There is a lovely atmosphere in that home,' observed Marjorie Nowell, sister-tutor at Saiburi, after she had paid them a visit. And in one of her letters Margaret wrote that she could not have been put with anyone she loved more or got on with better than Minka.

Their attitude towards the leprosy work was dominated by the unalterable conviction that God had called them to it. It was something that must be done, whatever the hardship entailed or the risks run in visiting patients in remote rural areas.

'I was taken yesterday to see a lady who had recently been shot,' wrote Margaret in one of her letters home. 'Three of the group she was with were killed. It was a forceful reminder to me of the unrest there is around us.' She noticed that the boatmen who took them to the fishing villages were always impatient to get away about noon. Minka realised the dangers, too. When Alan Ellard returned to his home in Khuan one day when Minka was there, and mentioned having gone to a village where he'd heard shots fired to see if anyone was hurt and needed help, she scolded him soundly for having done it. 'You ought not to go to such dangerous places,' she said. 'Think of Maelynn and the children! What about them, if anything happened to you?' But when Jit, who sometimes accompanied her and Margaret on their country visits, remonstrated with them for going so far off the well-frequented highways, their answer was, 'Yes, we know there is danger. But you have to think of it in this way—if we don't go to those people so ill with leprosy, what will happen to them?'

'They'll die,' Jit admitted. He remembered the time when he himself had expected to die.

'So you see if we leave them and they die, aren't we to blame?'

'You look after others better than you look after yourselves,' said Jit, who later related, almost in tears, how he had seen them in the rainy season wading through mud and water, 'slipping and sliding kilometre after kilometre to visit the sick. Margaret and Minka were foreigners in our country,' he went on, 'but these are the loving deeds they have done for us. Such goodness as this should be inscribed in the hearts of all Thai people!'

As 1973 was drawing to a close Minka, as usual, wrote a letter to be duplicated and sent to her many friends. She was very busy, and it was obviously produced rather hurriedly. Her vivid descriptions of checking a chapter of Acts with Uncle Mat and witnessing the baptism of leprosy patients in a river contained no carefully prepared phrases. There is no reason to believe she wrote under a solemn sense of prophetic foresight when, instead of concluding with the words 'As Christmas is fast approaching I would like to wish you all a very happy time and much blessing in the New Year,' she went on unexpectedly,

'How comforting to know that the Lord is in control in these troubling times.' But in the light of what happened afterwards it is difficult not to believe that Another was guiding her hand when she added:

For 1974: 'Thou dost show me the path of Life
            In Thy presence there is fulness of JOY!
            At Thy right hand are pleasures for
                evermore!'
                        Yours in this wonderful God,
                        Minka Hanskamp

The Mission Home in Yala was alive with guests and animated chatter. The South Thailand Field Conference was getting under way, with missionaries arriving from Satun, Pattani, Narathiwat, Khuan and Saiburi for the four days of fellowship and discussion held every year, at which they met together as a team. The Pink Palace, as it was called because of the colour of its walls and the rather uncomfortable size of its rooms, was the centre to which everyone naturally gravitated, though the meetings were held in the more austere surroundings of the Students' Hostel. Meals out in the garden under the trees added to the sense of festivity, and if sleeping conditions were somewhat crowded, with beds made up in corridors, no-one seemed to mind.

The programme of the Conference included gatherings for prayer and discussion in which all took part, but a guest speaker had been invited to lead the main devotional meetings each morning, and as he announced his subject, Christ as the Servant whose portrait emerges so glowingly in Isaiah, Margaret's attention was arrested.

The Servant. The Suffering Servant. The emphasis to her was on the suffering. It was a subject that had come often to mind during the past two years when she had been deliberately spending more of her spare time waiting on God. There was nothing in her immediate circumstances to account for it, for although the leprosy work was hard, in her personal life she was happy. 'I am grateful for good health and enjoyment in the work here,' she had written quite recently. There was no explaining why, during her autumn holiday in the hills of North Thailand, she and her friend there had both become aware as they were praying that it was the last time they would be together in this way. It had had a solemnising effect on both of them, the sense of impending separation. With a colleague too, at Saiburi, down by the lagoon where they had gone early one morning to share some problem together, had come in the stillness the consciousness of the Presence of the One they were seeking. It had been a sacred moment as they had sensed, not seen, He was holding out a cup towards them, and that it was a cup of suffering. 'The cup that My Father giveth me, shall I not drink it?' The quiet reminders had come, through the last two years, that the disciple of Christ must be prepared for separation, for suffering, and now it had come again, through the lips of His servant.

'Jesus did not heal the sickness of sin by some word of power, but by taking it to Himself, bearing it, and so destroying it,' said the speaker, and went on, 'The ultimate triumph came through rejection—affliction—bruising—and death.'

The application was obvious. The way of the cross offered no spectacular victory, no dramatic deliverance. What it offered was something deeper, richer. It offered fellowship with Christ in His sufferings, a fellowship that would endure when the sufferings were over, an intimate, tender relationship that nothing could surpass, that would make even glory itself more glorious.

On Sunday evening the Conference meeting took on a somewhat different character, and those who had a personal spiritual experience to share with the rest had the opportunity to do so. Margaret was almost the last to get to her feet, but eventually she stood up, saying how much the messages on the Suffering Servant had helped her, as the subject was one about which the Lord had spoken to her frequently over the past two years. Then she went on to say that in quiet moments during that period the Lord had spoken to her so clearly that she had written out His messages as they had come to her. She felt she could share one or two of them now, and opening the little notebook she had in her hand, she started to read.

> My child, I desire your love
> More than anything else that you can give Me
> Not your service
> Not your struggling and trying
> to please Me
> or to please others.
> I want you to love Me
> To love Me with all your
> heart
> soul
> mind
> strength.
> This is the first commandment
> and matters more than all else beside.
> I need your love,
> fellowship, devotion and worship.
> I want you to be single-minded
> in this one thing.
> My Spirit is within you
> to enable you
> to empower you

to fill your heart with love.
I desire this not sometimes
but always
Not part of the day
but all the day.
I'm more concerned with your love for Me
than what you do for Me
or do not do . . .
Remember my words to Peter
'Do you love Me?
Do you love Me more than these?'

It was somewhat of an emotional strain for Margaret to share such an experience with a group. She always found it much easier to confide her mystical experiences with the ones or twos whose devotional exercises took a similar form to her own, or whom she knew would understand. But on this occasion the inward compulsion to tell the whole group was so strong she could not refrain. 'I knew it was the Lord,' she admitted to one of her colleagues who came to her afterwards, asking permission to copy the message. 'I tried to put it off, but I knew I would have no peace if I didn't obey. So I did it.'

Shortly after the Conference Minka went away for two weeks, and Margaret was left alone. In addition to the keeping of accounts and records, and all that was involved in the leprosy work, she had responsibilities in helping younger missionaries with their language study, and arranging courses. And the car used for the leprosy work was always breaking down!

'I appreciate your concern for me, but don't be over-anxious, will you?' she wrote to her mother. 'The Lord keeps telling me to *trust* Him, and this is so necessary.' She admitted having many things on her mind however, and that she was getting tense and losing her sleep as a result.

Minka returned from her short holiday with a very heavy cold, and she had things on her mind, too. The task of translating the New Testament into the local Malay dialect was going ahead, and her part was to check it. She spent hours with Uncle Mat and others, the latest piece of translation in her hand, asking them to explain exactly what it said to ensure that the meaning was clear. There were patients who needed constant massaging, too, to bring life back to the withered muscles, and others who must be persuaded to work with their stumps of hands weaving baskets or making mops—anything to restore independence and self-respect. 'We must make a *man* of him!' she would say passionately. 'Not just leave him a whining beggar, waiting for hand-outs!' She went to infinite trouble, personal expenditure of time and money to devise ways to encourage leprosy patients who had lost hope to try and earn their own living. The rough baskets they made were beautified by the gay linings she sewed in them herself, and the customers were donors who had enrolled after hearing her speak when on furlough. Money seemed forthcoming easily enough for all aspects of the leprosy work—a new car had already been provided which was easing travelling—but where were the physiotherapists and occupational therapists whose work she was doing in addition to her own?

'I'd love to come and spend a weekend with you and the children,' she told Maelynn. 'But there's so much to do, I can't spare the time.' She longed for a few hours with the little ones. She loved being with children. When a letter had arrived in all the South Thailand centres from the school for missionaries' children in Malaysia, asking for a volunteer to help there over a certain period, Minka had responded eagerly. 'Wouldn't it be lovely if I could be there when Alison and Brenda arrive?' she exclaimed as she told Maelynn of her offer. But it could not be accepted, for there was no-one to replace her in the leprosy team during the specified period, and Minka relinquished the dream.

It was about this time that Minka read something which impressed her so deeply that she passed it on to a friend in one of her letters. The significance of it was to be evident very soon now.

'O My child, do not expect the trials to be lighter than in the past. Why should you think the testings would be less severe? Lo, I prove all things, and there are areas in your life I have not touched as yet. Do not look for respite. The days ahead may well call for greater endurance and more robust faith than you have ever needed before. Welcome this—for you must surely know by this time how precious are the lessons learned through such experiences. If it is not fully possible to anticipate them with joy, it is certainly not difficult to gain an appropriate appreciation afterwards in retrospect. Apply thine heart to learn with them. This goal transcends every other aim and any good that comes out of a pressure period is an added blessing in excess. Seek Me above all else.'

Good Friday came. It had been arranged that special meetings should be held at the Malay centre, when part of the film *King of Kings* portraying the crucifixion and resurrection of Jesus Christ would be shown. Minka had been chosen to re-tell the story on Easter morning, applying its message, a task from which she shrank. She would so much rather sit down with a small group in an informal way than stand before a waiting congregation to preach a sermon. 'Oh, Lord, deliver her from fear . . . speak through her in a special way today . . . Lord, help her!' Her fellow missionaries, who knew how she felt, prayed urgently. In addition to her natural nervousness her voice was badly affected by her cold, and when the time came for her to speak the microphone was handed to her with some trepidation. Would she be able to make herself heard?

But as she started to tell the crucifixion story all doubts vanished. 'It was thrilling to see her. She just acted the parts and made us enter into the feelings of those present at the crucifixion and resurrection. She was far more dramatic and gripping than the film, although I would have not thought this possible,' wrote one of those present, adding

that Minka did not stop at telling the facts, but made appli-
cations in a way that startled the hearers.

'Why did Judas betray Jesus?' she demanded, then
pointing her finger at first one, then another in the audience
cried with dramatic emphasis,

'Because of money—money—money!' There had been
some trouble over money among the residents at the Malay
centre, creating a delicate situation that no-one knew how
to deal with. It began to resolve itself that morning, as Minka
stood before them crying warningly, in a way some would
never forget,

'Money! Money! Money!' As she came to the resurrection and the scene in the garden there was the same
intensity of expression when she reiterated the words of
Christ to Mary,

'Go and tell My brethren. Go and tell! Go! Go! Go!'

When it was over she went to the kitchen to help with the
food that was to be served, and one of her colleagues, deeply
moved, came and whispered to her, with tears in her eyes,

' "Well done, thou good and faithful servant!" ' Minka
turned and smiled at her. 'The Lord just took over,' she said
simply, and went on with her serving.

Three days later she was at the Palas clinic. 'Wednesday
—the best day of the week for me,' she had said when she
first started going there to help Brenda at the commence-
ment of the leprosy work, and she still looked forward to
going, for on that day she was likely to get a glimpse of
the Ellard children. Their mother always tried to bring them
along, all five of them if possible, to see Auntie Minka. On
this particular Wednesday however Minka had an additional
reason for wanting to see Maelynn. There was something
she wanted to show her.

'Maelynn, look at this!' she said when she saw her, holding in her hand a printed newsletter. It was the November/
December 1973 issue of *Open Doors*, a periodical she received from time to time containing information about
Christians in the Soviet Union. 'I want you to ask the

Christians in Khuan to pray. Look, here is news of twenty-eight men behind the Iron Curtain who have just been tried and given long sentences of imprisonment, because of their faith in Jesus Christ. Look here are their names, their ages, the length of their sentences, some of them to hard labour. They are suffering for Christ's sake, and we ought to pray for them. Take it and tell the group in Khuan. Ask them to pray for those men. They're brothers in Christ!'

Maelynn was impressed by her earnestness. She was obviously passionately concerned about those men in the Soviet Union whom she had never met, but whose allegiance to their Master was leading them along the path of suffering. Maelynn looked at her friend, then her eyes dropped to the paper in her hand and she read the text that was on the top of the page.

'Don't forget about those in gaol. Suffer with them as though you were there yourself. Bear the sorrow of those being mistreated, for you know what they are going through.'

You know what they are going through. Minka had been through it herself, during those years in concentration camp. Had the memory of those experiences welled up again? Was that why her sense of involvement with those prisoners in the USSR was so acute? Or was there some other reason, a foreboding which she herself did not understand?

On the following night a shudder of alarm went through the area around Pujud, for there were unmistakable sounds of firing in the hills. The sound went on for a long time.

'Bandits die in clash!' ran the headlines in the *Bangkok Post* next day.

'Por Su says no surrender yet!'

The south was in the news. Newspaper reporters were on the alert. 'Yala—the city that lives in fear!' made an arresting title to an article in one of the English language papers, and was backed up by 'Bandits kidnap four from Yala!'

Ian Murray, Superintendent of the South Thailand OMF team, lived in Yala, in the Pink Palace. When he had been appointed to the position he and Vida had moved there from North Thailand where they were accustomed to alarms. There had been plenty of them in the mountains that bordered Laos and Burma, elaborated by hair-raising rumours which he had learned to pay no attention to until they were confirmed. However, there had undoubtedly been an increase in terrorist activities lately, and when he was over in Saiburi he had an informal talk about it with some of the missionaries there. Somehow he felt rather uneasy. He wasn't particularly anxious or apprehensive that anyone would be attacked in the towns or on the main roads, but Alan Ellard and Russell Gray were always off on their bikes to remote villages, and the leprosy nurses, when they weren't at the clinics, were likely to go away off the beaten track.

He decided to write to Isaac Scott, Director in Bangkok, and to HQ in Singapore. 'If anything should happen to our missionaries what is our policy, and how should we act in an emergency?' That was the main question he asked, and he posted the letter on Monday, 22nd April.

He did not know that the day before a stranger, a friendly young man, had visited the clinic in Pujud and enquired when the nurses were next due to come. If he had known he would not have given the matter a second thought. People frequently came to make such enquiries. Hassan did not give it a second thought, either. He was accustomed to such enquiries, and welcomed them. It gave him a feeling of some importance to be in a position to tell people when the clinic would be open and when they could come and see the nurses.

'On Tuesday, at nine o'clock,' he said. 'You'd better come early if you want to register. We get a lot of people here.' The young man nodded pleasantly and sauntered off. The message was sent to the teacher in the Islamic School who had left Pujud and gone to the hills . . .

So 23rd April, 1974 dawned. Exactly sixteen years before, to the very day, the door had opened to Minka to South Thailand. That may be why, with her orderly mind and memory for anniversaries, she brought her account book of personal expenditure right up to date. There was no time to spend thinking about it, for there was something she must do before she set off with Margaret for the Pujud clinic.

'That book Marjorie asked me for— we haven't got it here,' she said after looking through the book shelves. 'She wants it in time for her lectures to the aides on Friday. I wonder if this one will be any help . . .' It was typical of Minka that if she could not do exactly what was requested, she did the best she could. She pulled the book from the shelf and scribbled a note to Marjorie Nowell:

> Dear Marjorie,
>   This goes in haste.
>   We do not have any book here and I wonder whether David or someone else has them in their house. This book is all I have. Sorry!
>   Love,
>   Minka.

She was just about to seal it up when she remembered Chern. Chern, a friend of Jit, also had leprosy, and he was going blind into the bargain. A pair of dark glasses might help him, and she had a pair. So she added:

'P.S. Would you please ask Juppy to give these glasses to Chern? He is in the Malay centre.'

She put the things together in a little package and went quickly down the lane to the rank of gaily-coloured taxis at the end. There was always a taxi going to pick up patients for Saiburi hospital, and today was no exception. 'Will you hand this in at the hospital, please?' she said, giving the package to the driver, then back she went to the house to help Margaret load the things they needed into the car. It was all routine work. They had done it innumerable times before. They picked up the enamel basins, and the bundles of bandages made from old sheets, the scissors, the scalpels, the dressing forceps; gauze, adhesive plaster; the leprosy drugs in their containers, and for patients allergic to them, alternative medicines. Vitamins. Pain killers . . . All were packed neatly into the navy blue midwives bag they used for the purpose.

Russell Gray, who lived a little farther up the lane, had strolled down to see them off. The car had skidded and gone into a ditch a few days previously, when Margaret was at the wheel, and the reason was thought to have been too much air in the tyres. He took a look at them, then stood back as the two familiar figures in their sarongs and blouses clambered into the car, grinning as he saw Minka take her place behind the steering wheel. He had been teaching her to drive, and a very nervous pupil he had found her. 'Oh, Mudder!' she had exclaimed every time she did something wrong. But she had been determined to master the art of driving so that she would not be dependent on someone else to take her to her leprosy assignments. She had always cycled before, but her back was becoming too painful—and the car would enable her to do twice as much with half the effort. So she had persevered, and after two months Russell had thought it safe to apply for a licence for her and now, for almost the first time, she was in control of the vehicle.

'You sure look confident this morning!' he murmured as the car moved slowly away, and turned cautiously into the main road. Minka took no risks, and rarely went at more than twenty miles an hour.

The tarmac road ran through thickly wooded country, bamboos and evergreens on either side as they drove out of Pattani town. A lorry or two carrying white-ish sheets of rubber passed them, an overloaded bus, several taxis bulging with people. A few bicycles. It was only a journey of five or six miles, but as they drove into Pujud with its houses and shops on either side of the road, chickens, goats, ducks waddling about, they knew they were already later than usual. Should they go on to see if Fiona wanted a lift to the clinic? She and Sieglinde Frei had only moved into the house near the main street three weeks before, and although Fiona would be sure to come to the clinic to listen to Malay being spoken and pick up what new words she could, no definite programme had been established yet. She might already have gone there—in any case, it wouldn't take her more than five minutes on her motor-bike. Better go straight on to the clinic.

They turned into the shady lane, so familiar to them now, so near to the well-frequented highway. Everything was just as usual, a naked child and a woman in a sarong outside a house, a man strolling along the lane, ducks quacking beside a dirty little pool, a little group of people lounging around outside the clinic, waiting for it to open. A dark green Mazda taxi was cruising slowly past—probably bringing patients . . .

Minka and Margaret reached the clinic, responded smilingly to greetings, and started to get things ready, opening the bag with the medicines, getting out the register. The green Mazda car came to a standstill, and three men got out. Hassan, on the lookout for new patients, recognised one of them. It was the smiling young man who had come on Sunday to ask when the nurses would be coming, and Hassan moved towards him. 'Oh, you've come. It's good that you're early . . .' Then the words froze on his lips. The young man was not smiling now, and the warning look he gave to Hassan was reinforced by something he held in his hand, and that was pointing towards him. 'Don't you move, or . . .'

The other men were in the open-fronted clinic, pushing past the straggling bystanders, speaking peremptorily to the nurses.

'Come along with us. We want you to look after some sick people . . .'

It was not an unusual request, and they remonstrated casually that they must see the leprosy patients first. Then, if there was time, one of them would go . . .

'No. Come now. Bring your medicines, both of you, and come!'

Suddenly everything was silent. The straggling bystanders fell back, turned away. The men's attitude was menacing now, and there was no doubt as to what was happening.

Minka and Margaret started putting the medicines back into the case.

It was all over in a minute. As they walked out of the clinic Margaret tried to make a dash for the leprosy car, but of course it was useless. They were both pushed down into the taxi, sacks put over their heads, the engine roared and the Mazda shot off along the lane and out of sight.

On the very same day, in London, Brenda Holton, third member of the South Thailand leprosy team, received her medical clearance and was told she could return to the field.

CHAPTER EIGHT

SOUND THE ALARM!

From Margaret Morgan's notebook

My ways are
divergent, different,
They sometimes lie through the seas,
seas of trouble, sorrow,
anguish of spirit.
Sometimes through the wilderness
and dryness, and barrenness
and temptation.
Sometimes through dark valleys
and doubt and despair
and seeming defeat.
But there are always
the green pastures
the quiet places
where I feed and nourish
revive and restore
renew and refresh
your spirit.
Whatever the place
Wherever you find yourself
Remember My child that I am with you
to guard, to guide
to shed light on the road
to lead you in ways of righteousness
for your blessing
and for My Name's sake.

M.M.

At a dry time spiritually

FIONA LINDSAY LOOKED at her watch and saw it was ten minutes to nine. 'They won't be coming here now,' she thought. 'It's too late. They'll have gone straight to the clinic. They'll come back here when it's finished and we'll have our cup of coffee then.' She looked round the room to make sure everything was in order, closed the doors and shutters, then went upstairs to get ready to go to the clinic herself. She changed her sarong for one that was more suitable for riding on a motor-bike, then went over to the cupboard and reached on top for the two huge de-hydrated spiders she'd put there. Minka wanted them for the nephew of a friend of hers and Fiona had undertaken to provide them. 'I'll take them along with me, and that serviette ring of Margie's,' she decided. 'Just in case they haven't got time to call in afterwards.'

She was running a comb through her hair when she heard a man's voice outside, calling her name. There was an urgent ring about it, and when she looked out of the window she saw Hassan standing there. He started talking in a quick, agitated voice, and although Fiona had been studying the Malay language for only four months, she got the gist of what he was saying. 'The bandits—they've taken Minka and Margaret . . . please come right away!'

The next few hours were indelibly printed on Fiona's memory, although at the time she was so stunned by the news that she felt as though she was moving in a dream.

She got on her motor-bike and followed Hassan on his bicycle back to the clinic, past the dilapidated house she and Sieglinde Frei had nearly decided to rent a month ago. Not until later did the thought come of what might have happened if she had been in that house alone—or if she had gone to the clinic fifteen minutes earlier . . .

A group of people stood outside the clinic, dismay on their faces. 'They said they wanted the nurses to look after someone who was ill,' she was told when she asked what had happened. 'They made them take their medicines, then they went off at a terrible rate down the lane . . . Don't know which way they turned off . . . Don't know where they've taken them . . . Didn't notice the number plate, but they went off in a Mazda taxi—a green Mazda taxi . . .'

'I must let Ian know!' she thought. 'Go to Pattani and telephone from there . . .' But Hassan had collected his wits by this time, and said he must go and tell the headman before anything else and then they must notify the police.

'Of course—notify the police.' She waited for him to return from the headman, then he got on the back of her motor-bike and went to the Yarang police station, some five miles along the road. Once inside Hassan, who had been prepared to do all the talking until now, suddenly went silent. The police were Thai, and he was Malay. So Fiona, to whom the Thai language was no problem, told the story as best she could, not having been present at the kidnapping. She had to repeat it about half a dozen times, because as the gravity of the situation became apparent to each official she told it to, he said, 'You must see my superior officer.' When eventually she reached the man at the top, she put in her own urgent request.

'Please will you phone to our Mission Superintendent, Mr Ian Murray, in Yala? It's most important that he should know immediately,' and she gave the name and address, then asked if she could leave now to go to Pattani.

Yes, they would phone Mr Murray—yes, it would be all right if she left now. She got on her motor-bike, back through

Pujud, back over the road Minka and Margaret had driven along in the leprosy car only two hours before, back to the lane where they lived, and on to the Russell Grays' house.

'Russ is out,' said Enid, white-faced, as Fiona told her what had happened. 'He went off on his motor-bike soon after the girls did—I don't know where. He was going to some Malay villages somewhere in the backwoods. I don't expect him back for hours. Oh Fiona—Margie and Minka...!'

They stood together and prayed. Lord, look after them! Heavenly Father, keep them from evil. Oh, bring them back soon, bring them back safely. Lord, show us what to do...

'I felt I must let you and Russ know,' said Fiona. 'But I'll go back to Pujud now.' If Ian did not arrive soon, she'd go on to Yala, in case for some reason the news had not reached him. On her motor-bike again, back to Pujud, then on the twenty miles to Yala. 'They went off in a green Mazda taxi . . .' She passed at least a dozen Mazda taxis on that journey, in differing shades of green. 'I wasn't really frightened but—I felt a bit funny!' she admitted later, and felt thankful when, on entering Yala, she saw Ian coming out of the Telegraph Office.

'The wires were down so the police couldn't get me on the phone,' he told her. 'So they phoned Saiburi, then they sent a man round to let me know. I've just been confirming it with the police in Yarang. I'm going over there now. I reckon this is all the outcome of that big gun battle last Thursday night,' he went on. 'Some of the bandits were wounded, so they've probably taken the girls to look after them. They'll let them go after that.' Ian, tall, strong, confident, looked at Fiona and smiled. 'You'd better go and have lunch with Vida,' he said. Fiona had lived with them in North Thailand when first she arrived there as a new missionary, and they knew her well. 'Tell her all you know, and I'll push off to Yarang to see what can be done. Then I must phone Isaac Scott in Bangkok.'

The next day he went to the hospital at Saiburi. The dismay with which the news had been received there was alarming. Distress over Minka and Margaret, so well-known to everyone, only intensified the expressions of opinion as to what ought to be done.

'The hospital should be closed in protest,' said one of the Thai staff. Two or three years previously all the school teachers in the province had gone on strike because some of their number had been kidnapped, and security had been strengthened as a result.

'But we're in a different position,' explained Ian. 'We're guests in the country not citizens. It's not up to us to try to bring pressure to bear on local situations.' The *Principles and Practice* which all the missionaries had signed made that plain.

> Every member of the Mission must fully understand that he depends for help and protection on the Living God and does not rely on any human authority. While free to avail himself of any privilege offered by a government, he must make no demand for help or protection, though in emergencies he may need to ask for it.

Some suggested a partial closure—not enough to jeopardise the lives of any seriously sick people, but enough to affect public opinion further against the banditry.

Others were against any closure at all. Let there be show of neither fear nor retaliation. In the end, after discussing the situation fully and praying for God's guidance, Ian told the gathered company that he felt they should continue as usual, looking to the Lord to vindicate His own cause and to restore Minka and Margaret to them in His own way.

'There seems every likelihood that when the bandits discover they can't do anything in the way of getting bullets out, since they haven't got the right instruments with them, they'll let them go. It doesn't look like the usual sort of kidnapping—there's been no ransom demand.'

There was, indeed, a firm conviction on the part of all the

missionaries that Minka and Margaret would soon be released. God would hear and answer prayer—'Lord, for the
glory of Thine own Name, bring them back! Heavenly
Father, watch over them, provide for them, let their captors
soon release them. Lord, they are Thy children, Thy servants—let Your power be seen in delivering them!' They
made plans as to how they would look after them, what they
would do to help them get over the shock. They speculated
as to how they would be released—'probably at night, and
almost surely in a quiet place where no-one will see. Near
the hospital probably. The quiet lagoon and the uninhabited
stretches beyond would make it easy for the bandits to set
the girls down there and then get away.' So they had a room
prepared with the beds made up, and new towels and tooth-
brushes and soap all ready for use. The prayer meetings
were frequent and urgent, but when they were over, 'We'll
be having a great praise meeting before long!' Fiona, travelling between Pujud and Yala, found herself looking hope-
fully down every lane leading off the highway, half expecting
to see Minka's tall familiar figure, with the petite Margaret
beside her, walking towards her.

Meanwhile, in the homelands, news of the kidnapping
had spread in Mission circles. Alice van Zweeden, Minka's
sister in New Zealand, heard it announced on the radio as
she was preparing breakfast, and immediately the telephone
lines were humming. Not only there and in England and
Holland, where there was natural personal anxiety for the
two nurses, but in North America where neither of them
was known there was an immediate response when a news
item in a paper caught the eye of a missionary.

'As soon as we knew it to be a true report we alerted those
on our special mailing list, friends who pray for any urgent
need that may arise from whatever field—and of course all
members of the home staff throughout the country, retired
workers, and all Prayer Group leaders . . . from friends of
the Mission we heard of special prayer meetings being held

to pray for the girls, others who prayed for them at every
meal time, and so on.'

With such a widespread volume of prayer ascending spontaneously from so many people faith rose high and looked
for an immediate deliverance.

Then, exactly a week after the kidnapping, an envelope
was delivered at the Pink Palace, addressed to Ian Murray,
containing two letters. One was from Minka and Margaret,
and behind its opening phrase lay who could tell what of
quiet resistance and prayer for wisdom that they might
comply with the demands of their captors and yet write
nothing to deepen anxiety or make emotional appeals for
'deliverance at any price'. The letter stated simply,

Dear Ian,
    We have been told to tell you,
1. That we have been taken by the 'jungle people'.
    That we are safe and well, Margaret and Minka.
2. They are enclosing a letter with this one. They will tell
    you what they want in that letter.
3. We are well and provided for.
They are allowing us to write to our mothers today to tell
them what is happening. Whether they will arrive safely
or not we do not know. We have a long walk ahead of us
today.
    May the Lord clearly guide you. Still praising.
                    Minka. Margaret.

Ian opened the other letter quickly, and his face became
grave as he read it. Briefly, it made two demands. One was
for the payment of ten million baht, and the other that protests against the Israelis should be written officially by the
Overseas Missionary Fellowship.

This was more serious than anything he had imagined. It
brought the whole affair into the realm of international
politics, the explosive situation between Israel and the
Arabs. Neither demand could be met, of course. There was

no question about paying a ransom. To do so would be to put a price on the head of every missionary—and every missionary's child—in the country. Even if the demand had been a reasonable one the answer would have been the same, though £200,000 put it beyond consideration anyway. But what of Minka and Margaret now? All hopes that they would soon be released, that they had been taken merely for the purpose of tending the wounded, were gone. Although when Ian discussed the matter with officials they assured him that it was very unlikely any harm would be done to the two captives, they also admitted it would probably be a very long time now before they were eventually released unless some unexpected grounds for negotiations were found.

The whole situation had taken on a grimmer, more malevolent aspect. The ominous question arose 'Who next?' and on the same day as he received the letter Ian went to bring Fiona, living alone in Pujud, to the Pink Palace in Yala, while the Ellard family with their five little ones were withdrawn from the vulnerable village of Khuan. Alan continued his journeyings around remote villages, but took the precaution of carrying what he called his 'jungle pack' with him. It contained, among a few bare necessities, a Bible and concordance so that he would have something worthwhile to study if he were held in a bandit hideout.

All the members of the South Thailand team were living in varying degrees of tension now, and it was with some trepidation that Denis Lane, Overseas Director of OMF, wrote to them:

'. . . fully conscious of the fact that away in Singapore I am not subject to the same daily pressures and atmosphere that surround you constantly. On the other hand, because of this emergency, Ian Murray, Isaac Scott and myself have the God-given responsibility to determine policy for our work . . .' He went on to draw an analogy between the circumstances of King Hezekiah as recorded in 2 Kings 18 and 19 and those forced on the Fellowship by the kidnapping, ending with the words:

' "That all may know that You are God alone." Is not this why we have come to South Thailand in the first place? Is this not what we have been telling people all along? God has placed you brethren in a position of great testing, but it can also be a time of great proving. The way we Christian missionaries act and react now may determine for many years to come what the people of South Thailand think of the Lord we would commend to them. Is He really alive and able to keep us in His peace in a situation of life and death, or does He fail when we need Him most? I may not face the dangers as you do, but believe me I face the test of faith.' Then, as his mind went back over what he had read of the perils faced by Hudson Taylor and his 'Lammermuir party' of new workers in hostile China, of the Yangchow riots and the Boxer uprising, he added, 'May God keep us in His confidence as He has kept many of our predecessors in even darker days in China.'

As to the policy to be adopted in the present situation, it was, to put it in a nutshell, 'No ransom—business as usual.' But it was made plain that 'anyone was free to withdraw from the South Thailand field to work elsewhere, without any reflection upon their dedication or standing within the Fellowship.'

No-one withdrew.

Although the missionaries themselves approved of the policy and were prepared to accept it, there were different reactions from others when it was known that no ransom would be paid. Feelings ran high in some directions because of what appeared to be a lack of concern for Minka and Margaret. Jit, for one, was very dissatisfied, and was all for going into the hills to look for them. 'One of my friends, Chern, has the same sort of disposition as me,' he wrote to Mrs Morgan later, 'namely we were cross with others in not going to follow our two elder sisters. For the first week I joined the others in praying for them at eight o'clock every morning, but afterwards I stopped because I thought they were only praying.' He and Chern talked about it together.

'Oh, if I only had my eyes and my feet like other people!'
said Chern bitterly. 'Even now I could find that gang if
someone went with me!' He had been in a gang himself
before blindness and leprosy struck him, and knew the
devious ways of the underworld. 'I'll go with you,' said Jit.
They'd go and find the gang, and if they couldn't rescue the
nurses they'd offer themselves as hostages instead . . . They'd
do anything . . . But eventually the futility of the plan became evident to them, and they returned to prayer with increased intensity.

Meanwhile Ian was learning how intricate and bewildering
was the network of intrigue that spread like a web over the
southern provinces, with gang politics and informers and
people who 'knew a man who said he knew someone who
was in touch with the gang that had the nurses'—and who
would be prepared to take messages to them for a little
monetary consideration. He discovered, too, how to discern
when a ransom demand note came from a false source. In
the three weeks following the arrival of the one that came
with the letter from Minka and Margaret he received four
more letters, some in Malay, some in English, from gangs
purporting to be the one that held the nurses. The first
of these was on official-looking paper headed with the
name of 'Liberation Front' which was couched in con-
ciliatory language but made further political demands. It
proved to be from a guerrilla group in quite a different area,
but in those early days it was taken seriously, and served to
confuse the issue. As with all such communications, he
passed it on to the police.

The first real gleam of encouragement came through an
interview he had with a high-ranking Thai official to whom
he expressed his earnest desire to get some message through
to the two nurses. The Thai official was working to bring
about peace in the disturbed province and promised to do
what he could through his 'secret service' to deliver what
Ian wanted to send. It was at this time, a fortnight after the
kidnapping, that he handed over what he knew they would

want more than anything else—a Bible. With it he passed on two mimeographed song books, and a letter from Minka's mother. Of the many parcels that were sent in by various means, this was the first of the few known to have reached its destination, and it elicited an immediate response. Again a letter came out of the mysterious jungle, though it had been posted in the border town of Sungei Golok. It was dated 18.5.74, and written by Minka in the same style as the first one.

Dear Ian,

Great rejoicing in receiving Bible and hymnbooks, somewhere there seems to be a letter too. Thank you very much.

1.   Margaret and I are taken by the Malay guerrillas in Pattani.

2.   We both are in good health we are told to write.

3.   Told to ask you to come to a decision quickly so that we can be freed. Told to ask you not to be silent.

Greetings in the Lord,
Minka.

There was a PS from Margaret scribbled at the end, which appeared to have been added without surveillance.

Hello. We are OK here. Looking forward to seeing you so much in His time. Thanks so much for the Bible which has brought much comfort.

Margaret.

The letter reached Ian on 24th May, the day before that which had been set aside for prayer and fasting for Minka and Margaret. He had something on his mind that day which he could not share with anyone. Only Isaac Scott in Bangkok knew that he had been in touch again with the friendly Thai official, and plans were afoot to arrange a meeting with the chief bandit of the gang that had kidnapped Minka and

Margaret. The Thai official, with commendable courage, had overcome his nervousness at the proposal sufficiently to go ahead with the arrangements, and Ian was to go with him to the appointed rendezvous in four days' time.

He knew it was a dangerous thing to do, and for that reason did not tell Vida until a couple of days before he was due to go. He did not want her to have the burden of it on her mind. Better for him to bear it alone. It was a relief when the day actually dawned, and he set off in a Land-Rover with the Thai official and three members of his staff to keep the appointment.

The instructions sent by the bandit chief had been firm and explicit. No word to the military. No guns. Only five people. Any breach of the agreement and there would be trouble! The place of meeting was on a lonely stretch of road near the jungle where there was a rough shelter, a *sala*, and as the car cruised up to it they saw an old man chopping wood some distance away. Apart from him there was no sign of life, though a few houses could be seen through the trees. The car cruised on for a mile or two, then turned round and came to a stop at the shelter. The old man heaved a log of wood on his shoulder and walked off towards the houses.

'We'd better get out,' said the official. 'Stand around, let them see us. You stroll over towards the houses,' he added to one of his staff. 'See if anyone comes to meet you.'

The man sauntered off, and when he had gone a few hundred yards the old man re-appeared with another man, coming towards him. A third man stepped out of the jungle and joined them. They stood talking together for a minute, then one of them beckoned to the little group at the *sala* to join them.

As they were being conducted towards one of the houses Ian noticed two or three armed men lurking in the trees. The bandits were taking no chances! And when they were led into an empty house to meet the chief, a younger man of under thirty, they saw that he had a pistol, too. He took it out of his pocket during the course of their conversation and laid it on the mat before him as they sat around, cross-legged on the floor. But he was friendly enough in his attitude, prepared to respond to the interest expressed by the Thai official as to his reason for being a bandit and an outlaw.

It had come about, he said, because a friend of his who felt the same way as he did about the right of the southern provinces to be independent was clamped in gaol and his wife assaulted. Fearing the same thing might happen to him and his own wife, they fled from Pujud, where he had been teaching in an Islamic school, and fell in with the Communist guerrillas on the Malaysian border. For two years he was with them, and they gave him good training in guerrilla tactics. He appreciated their training but not their ideology. They wanted him to give up his Allah and his fast days, and he intended to stick to both. So eventually he left them, and set up on his own, specialising in kidnapping. Why had he kidnapped Minka and Margaret? He had received his instructions from 'higher up' he said, from another gang, so he had no authority to release them. In any case, he had handed them on now.

Ian thought quickly. 'We have a long walk ahead of us today,' Margaret and Minka had written four days after they were kidnapped. Was that when they were handed on? And where did the walk end?

Understandably the young bandit was not prepared to divulge all he knew, though he told them a good deal. He was evidently in no position to release the two nurses but,

'If you'll help me, I'll try to help you,' he said.

'How can we help you?' the Thai official enquired, and the bandit told him. It was his wife. She wanted Thai citizenship. She was a Thai, had been born in Thailand, but for rather obvious reasons she could not appear to make her own request for the required certificate.

'I'll see if that can be arranged,' the official said, and drew out his notebook. Her name? Age? Place of birth? . . . He jotted the information down, and the bandit looked satisfied.

Now it was Ian's turn to speak, and there was only one line that he could take.

'About those two nurses,' he said. 'They are here for religious purposes. We missionaries are all here for religious purposes. *You* will understand that,' and the bandit nodded. It was on account of his own religion he had left the Communists. 'We worship the one True God, the Creator God, and you know about Him.' Again the acquiescent nod of the head—the Muslim owns only One God, unlike the Buddhist with his numerous dieties. 'We are hoping that you will understand that we too are serving this Creator God. This God will honour us, and there will be terrible judgment on anyone harming God's servants . . . But He is a God of mercy and forgiveness, as well as a God of judgment. He is ready to forgive you, but whether He does so depends on your response to Him . . .'

The bandit listened quietly. Whether or not he was affected by what was said was open to conjecture, but at any rate he was not enraged. He agreed to speak on behalf of the two captured missionaries to the one 'higher up', and promised to see that the little plastic container Ian had brought was delivered to them.

The official's party bowed quietly to the bandits, walked back to the Land Rover and drove back to Yala, not without a sense of relief that it was over. The young bandit not only had a gun in front of him as they talked, but, as they learned later, a hand grenade tucked into his loin-cloth.

One piece of information that had been gleaned in the course of the conversation was that the man controlling the whole affair of the kidnapping was living in exile. 'If only we could see him!' He was very wealthy and very inaccessible. However, they made the effort, which involved Ian doing some travelling and then spending half a night in the sort of club not usually frequented by missionaries. They met there a go-between who agreed to arrange a meeting with the big man himself in the not-too-distant future, and returned with reasonably high hopes that something would come of it.

Then events took an ominous turn, with a police unit being ambushed on the 'Death Highway' between Saiburi and Narathiwat. Military activity was intensified, forcing the bandit gangs deeper into the mountains. Smugglers took advantage of trouble inland to ferry arms across the Gulf of Thailand from Cambodia and South Vietnam. The south was making headline news in the Bangkok papers, and conditions there were reported as 'deteriorating'.

'Six More Armoured Cars for the South.'

'Terrorists Plan Retaliation for Govt. "Invasion".'

'Drive Traps Bandits.'

'Bandits Hit Back . . .'

Day after day the Bangkok papers had reports on what was happening, and on 4th June, a day that had been set aside throughout the OMF worldwide for prayer for Minka and Margaret, one of the reports ran:

'The kidnapper of two foreign women missionaries in the south told the Deputy Yala Governor last Wednesday that he would secure the release of the two hostages from his boss Poh Yeh in two weeks . . .'

The rumour was quickly fastened on to by the international press, and the following day a west country newspaper in Britain carried the news item that 'Welsh nurse, Miss Margaret Morgan . . . may be released in a fortnight.' Throughout the month of June rumours persisted in South Thailand that the two missionaries were freed.

They were in Pattani!

They were in Malaysia!

They were in Singapore!

At one stage the rumours were so emphatic that Ian was besieged by Thai officials and the Press for confirmation of the reports. Had he succeeded in making secret negotiations and smuggling the two captives out of the country?

What had actually happened was something very dif-

ferent. Word had come that the man whose help they had
sought would not see them. Furthermore, an influential
gang had written implying that they had no quarrel with the
OMF—it was from the Governments of the USA and the
UK that the ransom money should come. They further
demanded that:

'Christian world should stop any support to Israel against
Palestinian people' and 'All Christian nations must strongly
oppose any oppression and inhumanity to the Palestinian
people'. Letters outlining the same demands were also sent
to Mrs Hanskamp in Holland and Mrs Morgan in Wales.
Photographs taken of Minka and Margaret sitting together
in a jungle setting authenticated the communications. The
kidnapping of the two nurses had ramifications far beyond
the local situation in South Thailand.

The news departments of the mass media got hold of the
story and interpreted it in their own way. Well-wishers in
England urged that the matter should be brought up in Parliament, that 'something ought to be done about it'. 'Informed sources' in Asia said that the UK was taking a hand
in affairs, and that the OMF had even been consulting with
the Singapore Government, a pure invention of some fertile
journalistic imagination. Memories of the early days of the
CIM's history came to mind, when British gun-boats had
steamed relentlessly up the Yangtse 'to do something about
it' as a result of news that had got through of the besieging
of the missionaries on their compound in Yangchow. The
grief and horror of the missionaries when they knew about
the action taken was far greater and more lasting than the
shorter-lived fear and pain they had endured during the
riots, and from which they had already escaped when the
matter came up in Parliament. The lessons learned then had
gone towards the thrashing out of those *Principles and Practice* in which it was emphasised that 'appeals to any official
to procure punishment of offenders or to demand the vindication of real or supposed rights were to be avoided', and
that each member must depend on the Living God, not on

any human authority. It was at His command that they had gone out, not at the instigation of any earthly government, and to Him alone would they commit their cause.

The implementing of this principle in 1974 when two women fellow missionaries were captives in an Asian jungle was not the easiest thing for men who had to stand firm on it. There would be those who would question the rightness of the attitude, especially if things went wrong. Yet there was no other course open to them. The ransom could not be paid.

On the human level there seemed only one thing that might free the nurses now.

'If two of us could take their places, do you think they might let them go?' said Denis Lane to Isaac Scott. 'I'd thought of that myself,' was the reply. 'And Ian has said he's willing to try. But all contacts have been lost and there seems no way of getting in touch.'

Ian and Vida were due to return home on furlough in August, but with Minka and Margaret's situation as it was, and Ian being the one who had all the contacts, he volunteered to delay his return to Britain.

Of course! It would mean a bit of an upheaval to family plans, but it could be arranged.

He had just heard of a man who had been taken blindfold to the bandits' hideout to pay protection money, to ensure that his family and home would not be molested. It was very primitive, he had told a relative in low tones when he returned. There was not much food in the camp. The men prisoners were in chains. While there he had seen the two foreign women. They were being kept in a fairly isolated situation, and had a bamboo bed with a tarpaulin covering. They were not in chains . . .

How accurate the report was Ian did not know, but it did not sound very reassuring. There were some things he kept to himself—better to carry the burden on his mind than let others be crushed by it. But in the circumstances it was easier to stay than to go. So while Vida and their eldest son, due to enter boarding school in England, went home, and

the two younger children said a tearful goodbye to Daddy
and Mummy and returned to Chefoo School in Malaysia,
Ian stayed on in Yala. 'It's the least we can do for Minka
and Margaret,' he said.

CHAPTER NINE

WAYS PAST FINDING OUT

From Margaret Morgan's notebook

I want you to trust Me, child,
This I have to tell you over and over again.
I want you to trust Me.
You ask how you may bring joy to My heart
How you may bring Me pleasure.
This is the way, My child,
by your trust.
Your complete and utter trust
in Me and in My way with you.
I long for you to be joyful too
I long for you to be unburdened
carefree, happy
My best for you is gladness
not sadness and gloom
a spirit oppressed.
This will only be as you are in Me,
abiding in Me,
loving Me, trusting Me.
With that complete and utter trust
of a child in her father.
Oh child, remember this
When you are tempted to be disturbed
lose your peace of heart
remember to trust Me
and recognise the subtle ways of the evil one
who seeks above all else to destroy
this trust, this rest
I would have you enjoy.
                          M.M.

IF THE POLITICAL issues of the kidnapping of Minka and Margaret apparently went no further than sympathetic concern in ambassadorial circles and appropriate action on the part of Thai officials, the spiritual issues were as widespread as the ripples on a pond when a stone is thrown in. The interest aroused went far beyond OMF circles. From quite unexpected sources came letters and messages telling of people gathering to pray for the release of the two missionary nurses, ranging from little boys in a preparatory school to members of a church in Holland where prayer meetings were not usually on the weekly programme. Believers in a small town in Brazil '. . . have realised perhaps for the first time the cost of following Christ,' and from a Christian woman in one of the Communist countries of East Europe came, with the assurance of her prayers, the significant phrase, 'God does wonderful works through the sufferings of men. We will see what He will do through the two nurses . . .'

Letters and telephone calls with the question, 'Is there any news of Minka and Margaret?' were frequently received at the headquarters of the Mission in the various home countries, and such information as was available was circulated widely. Expectation of their release continued high and prayer urgent as every conceivable aspect of their captivity was touched on.

'Lord, give them peace of heart, the assurance of Thy presence . . .'

'Give them adequate food . . . clothing . . . shelter . . .'

'Give them kindly captors . . . preserve them from assault on mind or body . . .'

'May they be kept together, Lord. Don't let them be separated . . .'

'Margaret has to be so careful about what she eats — don't let her have any digestive troubles . . .'

'Minka's back, Lord — ease the pain . . .'

'Oh, Lord, give them an early release. Bring them out soon . . .'

This urgent prayer for their release was the predominating one throughout the summer of 1974. Every bit of news that could be gleaned from the letters they were able to send out was lapped up eagerly. The first letter Mrs Morgan received from Margaret was on 1st May, and she did not know whether to laugh or cry as she read it.

27th April 1974
10 a.m.

My dear Mum, Elaine and Andrew,

I'm sorry the news is not so good this weekend. Minka and I were 'taken' at the Pujud Clinic 9 a.m. Tuesday this week.

They are allowing us to write to you to tell you and Minka's Mum that we are quite safe! We are provided for and are fit.

It will be difficult for you not to worry but I know the Lord will give you peace as He has given us. Pray for God's leading for Isaac Scott and others.

The men here want us to tell you that you are to give this news to the Government! !

God abundantly bless,

Lots of love,

Margaret

Minka's letter to her mother in Holland contained the same news and the same assurance.

'The Lord is very near. We praise and pray much, sometimes sing. We have enough to eat. Pray that they will never touch us. It is natural that you should be worried, but the Lord gives real peace every moment. Keep your eyes on Him. Ps. 91. He is very near and He is in control.'

Three weeks later on 18th May, the day after they received the Bible and hymn-books, they were allowed to write again.

'The one in charge wants me to tell you the following,' wrote Margaret. 'He doesn't want you to be distressed! You are to tell Mr Carr and the Government that they must come to some decision quickly!' and to that she added, 'This request is supposed to come from me. We are praying much that those in charge will really know God's will.'

Minka, for whom a letter from her mother had been included with the Bible, admitted,

'I must say I could not withhold my tears when I saw your letter in the hands of the man here,' and giving a little information about conditions, 'We have enough rice . . . a roof over our heads and God's protection.' It appeared that having nothing to do all day was the greatest trial. In no letter did they indicate they were called on for any nursing, although rumours persisted that this was what they were doing. 'We read the Bible *all* day' indicated clearly that it was their only occupation, and twice in the letters they sent to Ian they asked for paperbacks and magazines to read if there was to be any further delay, though 'If you could finalise these things very soon we would be so glad' wrote Margaret in the last letter he ever received. 'We just sit here all day.'

Surprisingly, the only reference made to any physical illness was in a postscript to one of the five letters written, one each month, to Ian. 'My main bother is my ear (left) — nasty infection,' Margaret had scribbled. 'Seem to be deaf on that side,' but later she reported, 'My ear is OK now.'

At the end of June they both wrote again. The address they gave, as always, was simply 'Jungle', but it was apparently in a different part, and it was from a hideout on a mountain that they were allowed to write to their mothers, giving as much information as they dared.

They were very high up, almost surrounded by rocks, but evidently above a main road for 'we càn hear the traffic below'. Every now and then they glimpsed some very beautiful flowers that no-one looked at, 'but that grow here all the same just for the joy of the Lord'. As for themselves, their home was a narrow bed with a rock face for a wall, and an awning of leaves for a roof. 'Our bed is our house— it is all we have.'

Their diet was rice and dried fish twice a day, and once a fortnight a piece of fruit. 'We are both thinner but reasonably fit.'

Clothes? They had been taken off in the sarongs and blouses they wore for the clinic work, and had nothing else with them but a few medicines. Four days after they were taken they were given combs, mirrors, tooth-brushes and tooth-paste and a pair of silk pyjamas and a sarong apiece. Also a sheet. They had received the sets of underclothing Vida had put in the plastic container for Ian to hand on when he met the bandit chief, although Minka and Margaret knew nothing of those circumstances. All they knew was that they had received sets of underclothing 'from outside'. They found an old sarong and trousers and a jacket. 'A kind fellow who was here gave me a shirt and a cotton jacket of his,' wrote Margaret. But up on the mountain it was often cold and there was much rain, and they had only a piece of tarpaulin for a covering. 'It is the Lord who keeps us from catching cold. He cares for us. Every night He protects us from animals.'

Sometimes they collected some leaves to make their bed softer.

Margaret had celebrated her fortieth birthday in those grim circumstances, but, 'I was almost overwhelmed . . . four days after my birthday I received what you sent with

Brenda plus a letter from Alma . . . I have read all the letters over and over . . . .'

'We have nothing to do here, there is no-one to be cared for. We just take turns reading the Word for an hour at a time . . . It is tremendous the way the Lord gives us His peace when we become discouraged so that we can sing and praise together.'

Margaret concluded her letter with the reference Colossians 1.11. Each of the letters, the longest they had written, contained messages to families and friends, although 'whether this letter will ever be sent I don't know, but the man said that we could write again.'

Their uncertainty was justified. Seven weeks were to elapse before the letters were eventually dispatched. During that time Minka and Margaret had been moved again, as they explained briefly in the postscripts they were permitted to add to the letters.

'We are still in the same situation though a different place. Please keep praying. As far as we know things are at a standstill . . .' The letters that Ian had written to them had not got through, though Margaret had received more letters from her mother containing, of course, only local news. Minka had received none. 'Maybe they have been held up somewhere,' she wrote, knowing that letters were opened, and that since no-one in the camp could understand Dutch any from Holland might have been confiscated. 'He is taking care for you and for us. Don't forget that, will you?' And Minka concluded her postscript with the same Scripture reference that Margaret had used at the end of her letter. Colossians 1.11.

14th August was the date of the postcripts, and it was on the same day that they were instructed to write to Ian. They were allowed to tell him of the letters Margaret had received three weeks previously, and that Minka wanted news of her mother, not having heard for two months. They told him they had received nothing from him, and asked him to send a raincoat and a flat rubber cushion for Minka, warm socks

and a thick cardigan for Margaret and 'books and magazines to read, as we have nothing to do all day'. But the
main purpose of the letter was obviously to provide a covering note for the leader's own demand.

'This is the *last time* that there is going to be a letter sent
from the head of this group,' was the first sentence written
and the letter ended, 'After writing the above it is suggested
we tell you again to settle things quickly.'

> Yours in Him,
> With many thanks,
> Minka.   Margaret.

The letters reached Ian a week later. He received them on
his return after driving a hundred miles to Narathiwat to
see an influential official who proved not to be there, and
driving the hundred miles back. If he had known he was
holding in his hand the last letters of Minka and Margaret
he could have done no other than what he did. The letters
they had written to their mothers were forwarded with a
covering note giving as much information as he could. As
for the answer to the demand, that could not change. It
remained the same. No ransom. No political involvement.

But as it was, he did not know he would never hear from
them again. He read their letter to him and observed rue-
fully that none of the things he had tried to send them had
got through. The marvel was, in the circumstances, that the
letters from Mrs Morgan in Wales had been passed on.
Margaret had received them, at any rate, even though nothing else had been delivered. Well, he'd have to go on trying,
for it looked as though those who prophesied it would be
a long business were right.

So the days of August passed, and September too, with a
spate of rumours.

The two missionary nurses had been shot, it was whispered, before Ramadan.

In direct contradiction came the evidence of a Chinese

merchant who had actually seen them when he himself was held for ransom in the camp. They were very thin, and troubled by mosquitoes, and had only dried bananas to eat, but were nevertheless alive.

Their conditions were not as reported! On good authority it was asserted that even during the fast of Ramadan they had been given coffee and Ovaltine to drink, and adequate food.

They had been seen on 1st October, and by village standards were living very well.

As for their whereabouts, they were deep in the Budo mountains . . .

October came and went, and still Ian's efforts to establish contact were unsuccessful. People were found who agreed to take letters, books, items of clothing, who had ways and means of getting them delivered to the nurses (for a price), but they never returned with any evidence that they had got through. In November harrowing reports appeared in leading British national newspapers to the effect that the missionary nurse from Wales, Miss Margaret Morgan, and her companion from New Zealand were being kept in chains by bandits in the jungle of South Thailand.

Through it all the missionaries in South Thailand continued outwardly as usual, proclaiming a Divine Saviour whose glorious resurrection was preceded by a death of suffering and shame, of whom it was said then that 'He saved others. Himself He cannot save . . .' But inwardly they carried a burden. Minka and Margaret were never far from their thoughts, always in their prayers, and when they gathered for their times of fellowship one hymn in particular was announced over and over again—a hymn in which by common consent one line was altered.

> Holy Father, in Thy mercy,
>   Hear our anxious prayer
> Keep our loved ones, Marg and Minka
>   'Neath Thy care.

Among the Thai and Malay Christians were some who perhaps felt the anxiety even more acutely than the missionaries themselves, for was it not on their account that Minka and Margaret had ever come to Thailand at all? Mrs Porn the inn-keeper, for instance. Mrs Porn was devoted to Minka, who had been her midwife in a difficult pregnancy, but she dismissed Minka's God with a shrug of her shoulders—until she heard that Minka had been taken by bandits. It was then that, with an anguished face, she sought her Christian husband and said, 'Oh, let us pray for them—pray for them *now*!' For Mrs Porn that was the step of faith that led her to Christ, and she was not the only one who came to Him as a direct outcome of what had happened. But the effect of the physical hardship Minka and Margaret were enduring, and the mental suffering of those who loved them best, was as wide and as indefinable as the fruitfulness of a field that has been fertilised. Nowhere was it more evident than in South Thailand. A new gentleness and mutual consideration characterised the relationships between the missionaries, a deeper note of devotion and dedication was apparent among the little groups of Thai and Malay Christians. With Minka and Margaret up there on the mountains, suffering for the sake of the Gospel of Christ, and Him crucified, it would be shame to anyone to hold on to imagined rights or petty grievances, to be afraid to confess Jesus as Lord.

During the autumn the tenor of prayer imperceptibly changed. Minka's brother in Australia realised that her widely-scattered family were praying now, not so much for her release as that she should glorify the Lord. Bert Taylor, minister of the Tabernacle in Porth in the Rhondda Valley, was conscious that at the weekly gatherings when Margaret was always remembered it was not so much the plea 'Lord, release her!' that was uttered as 'Thy will be done.' To accept the Father's will, whatever it might be, was the perfect prayer born out of the anguish of the human cry for deliverance, and here where those were who had loved

Margaret longest the prayer came from hearts that suffered for her. It was Bert Taylor's own prayer, too, when he prayed for her, but he was convinced that in this case the Father's will was deliverance, that one day Margaret and Minka would emerge alive and well from the jungle. Ever since the morning in October when he had awakened suddenly to say to Alma, 'We're going to hear soon that Margaret and Minka have been released,' he had been sure of it. What he had seen in a dream was etched unforgettably on his memory. 'Two figures, one tall, one short, walking away from me towards the light. I knew it was Margaret and Minka ... They're going to be released!'

But Mrs Morgan was not so sure. A few nights later she, too, had a dream. It was about Margaret. She was dying in a little hut in the jungle. The dream was so real, so vivid, she could not forget it for days, nor shake off the ominous portent of death.

She was not alone in this experience, though she did not know it. In Singapore, at OMF headquarters, Dr Monica Hogben woke at her usual time early one morning aware of something she could only describe as 'a horror of great darkness', and it was inextricably associated for her with Minka and Margaret. It was the time when she always prayed for them, but on this day it was an almost agonised cry on their behalf. After that the sense of concern for them passed away for ever. She found she could pray for them no more, 'only for their mothers, and the working out of God's will as a result of their lives laid down.' In Saiburi hospital one of the missionary staff was awakened one night with a deep quiet assurance that all was well with Minka and Margaret, and to the wife of one of the doctors came the same inexplicable conviction. In England one who was a stranger to both the captives nevertheless set herself to fast and pray every Thursday for them—but on the third Thursday the same sense of concern for them had gone. 'I seemed to hear the Lord saying "They are now in My immediate presence",' she told her husband and later a friend, but added, 'Don't mention it to anyone—sometimes we are deceived . . .' There were others, here and there, to whom the indefinable intimations came. Without authentic news, however, and mistrusting their own 'intuitions' they hesitated to assert what they themselves believed, and for the most part the volume of prayer continued unabated, although by the time January, then February of 1975 passed, and no news or even rumours for months, there began to be a sense of unreality about it. Perhaps that is why, in more than one place, the direct and urgent prayer burst forth, 'Oh, Lord, let us get authentic news.'

About the same time, in March, hope sprang up again in South Thailand. Quite unexpectedly it was reported quietly in official circles, that the two western women had been seen. They were alive, and in quite good health. It was so long since there had been any rumours about them, good or bad, that this was looked upon as a promising omen by those who were still praying and believing that Minka and Margaret would be restored to them.

Then on Thursday, 20th March, Denis Lane in Singapore was called to answer a phone call from Melbourne in Australia. 'Minka's brother has been in touch. He's heard that the bodies of two women have been found in the jungle in South Thailand. Can you confirm?'

No, Denis could not confirm. 'It's probably another rumour,' he said, but he put through a phone call to OMF headquarters in Bangkok. Yes, they'd heard it there, too, but it was unconfirmed.

Dr John Toop in Saiburi tuned in to the BBC news at seven a.m. as usual. Russell Gray, who happened to have spent the night with the Toops, was with him as they listened, suddenly electrified, to an announcement that the bodies of two women, believed to be the missionaries abducted by bandits last year, had been found in a jungle in South Thailand.

The two men looked at each other in dismay. 'We must find out for ourselves . . . Go to the police . . . Yala . . .' They got on Russell's motor-bike and went.

Some hours later, their faces grave, they returned to Saiburi.

Yes, it was true. The remains that had been found were those of Minka and Margaret. Identifying items found with them, little pieces of clothing, hair, dentures, left no doubt of it. But the forensic experts would take longer to confirm it to the satisfaction of the authorities, because what had been found by the police patrol in the hills five miles south of Yala, on the Raman road, were not actually recognisable bodies. Only bones, though the manner of death was quite clear.

In a stunned silence they explained there was conclusive evidence that Minka and Margaret had been shot through the back of the head five or six months ago.

CHAPTER TEN

THE WAY OF THE CROSS LEADS HOME

She was distressed
Disturbed
Brokenhearted
Because she couldn't find You.
'I don't know where you have put him,'
She cried.
She desired to see You again
Even though life was gone
And only a shell of a body remained.
Yet she loved You so much
And longed to bring You a gift
Just once more.
But her plans were frustrated
You were gone
The tomb was empty.

But You knew her desire
Her distress
Her deep love for You
and her tears.
So You come to her
To meet her in her need,
To turn her
Fear to faith
Grief to gladness
Darkness to light.
Instead of loneliness
Her Living Lord.

Thank You for Easter,
For the sunrise, sand and sea.
A new day
New life,
New hope
New awareness of Your person
New assurance of Your presence
New confidence in Your love.
Thank you that as You met Mary's need
So You meet mine.
Thank you for Your promise,
'I will not leave you comfortless,
I will come to you.'
                    M.M.

Easter Sunday

IT WAS TO the assembled missionary staff at the hospital that the two men first told the news, and the shock of it went all the deeper because of the recent reassuring rumour which had raised hopes that the long time of waiting was over, and the two nurses would soon be released. If one here and there in the group murmured, 'I felt sure they'd gone . . .', to the majority the tidings was totally unexpected.

'I was hard put to it to defend my faith in God', Russell Gray admitted later, 'it took me a full day to overcome the disappointment I felt'. And he was not the only one. 'In thinking of the death of Minka and Margaret we are faced with many conflicting thoughts and questions', Richard Dangerfield wrote frankly to his friends. It had been hard to take, the apparent failure of all the faith and prayer that had suffused the whole matter from the day of the kidnapping eleven months before. To talk about the blood of the martyrs being the seed of the Church is all very well when that blood was spilt a long time ago and a long way away. It is another matter when you've been praying every day for nearly a year that in this case your two colleagues won't be martyred at all, and fully expecting to receive what you've been asking for—the triumphant deliverance of the captives and the obvious vindication of faith.

The sorrow, too. It had subdued them like a mountain mist that muffles sound and obscures the view, for Minka and Margaret had been so much in their thoughts and prayers as to be almost more real than when they had been

there in person, just members of the team. Some of their
patients were obviously bowed with the sense of bereave-
ment, and Jit, in a letter to the mothers, said that when he
thought of Minka and Margaret,

> . . . it makes me feel sick at heart, as though something
> has pierced my heart, as though something has got
> stuck there. When I go to my rest, alone as always, I
> cannot help but think of them. Then I see the face of
> Minka who was always smiling, and as for Margaret,
> crossing the muddy rice fields to have communion with
> the family in Nongjig. My tears flow and then I go to
> sleep.
>
> Love and highest respects,
Jit.

It fell to Brenda Holton's lot to sort out the precious
personal belongings in the two bedrooms in the home in
Pattani, and she was overcome with emotion as the secret
things were revealed. Minka's patched sheets and simple
clothes and the carefully-hoarded old items she kept for
her own use, worn things that others would have discarded
long ago—but drawers full of generous presents ready to
be given away to others. And in the little account book in
which each item of expenditure was meticulously entered,
the words, 'Thank you, Lord', were written against every
record of money sent for her support.

Neatly stacked in little piles, all fresh and clean and
crisp were the clothes in Margaret's room—and there, too,
were found the simple exercise books in which she had
unconsciously breathed out the struggles and aspirations
of her heart, the ardour and devotion of her love for Christ.

There were evidences among their papers that neither
had gone into captivity without the forewarnings and
encouragements of God. Minka had kept a letter in
which something was written in prophetic vein that had
come to her with deep significance.

'O, my child, do not expect the trials to be lighter . . . The days ahead may well call for greater endurance and more robust faith than you have ever needed before. Welcome this . . . how precious are the lessons learned . . .'

In a notebook by Margaret's bed was a quotation from F. B. Meyer which she had written on a slip of paper shortly before she was kidnapped.

'Make no distinction between what God appointed and what God permitted. His permission and His appointments are equally His will. Now it seems to me as if you and I are enclosed in God. An arrow comes from the enemy's bow. If God liked, He could let the arrow pass through this way or that. But if my God opens and permits the evil to pass through His compassing power to my heart—by the time it has passed through God to me, it has become God's will for me. It is ever so much better for peace of mind to accept the will of God; to accept His permission and His appointment, to look up into His face and say, "Even so, Father." '

Gradually through the encompassing sense of sorrow there came a note of victory, sometimes very clearly and from unexpected quarters. Chern wrote to the two mothers expressing his grief that the two nurses would never again visit him, but was nevertheless quite sure that they had gone to God, and that He had 'arranged a place for them both all in order for them'. A little child sounded it, too, for Stevie Ellard went to his mother with an eager expression on his face and asked, 'Mummy, is Auntie Minka in Jesus' house now?' She had been afraid to tell him, fearing the effect it would have on his faith, but she need not have worried. There were no perplexities in his mind about unanswered prayer. He had prayed that Jesus would save Auntie Minka from the bandits, and Jesus had done it by taking her straight to His house—a place that had suddenly become real and warm and welcoming to Stevie, now that Auntie Minka was there.

Then there had been that strange experience of Mrs Morgan's two nights before she received the news that the bodies had been found in the jungle. She had dreamed again—but this time she was looking down a long, dark tunnel at the end of which she saw only radiant light . . . and a Throne . . . and Margaret was there . . .

Something could be divulged now, too, that all who had been watching and waiting would long to know. Early in the month of March a man had come forward with a story which at the time the missionary who heard it had not wanted to believe. The man had belonged to one of the Malay separatist gangs, but had surrendered to the police. He said that in September 1974 he had met a friend of his up in the hills who was a member of the very gang that had held Minka and Margaret, who told him what had happened to them.

'They're dead', he said. 'I shot them.' Then he went on to explain that there had been some discussion as to what to do with the two women. Some advised releasing them, others that they should be shot. They would just be a burden to the gang if they were kept indefinitely. Eventually the chief decided that, to keep the respect of the underlings, they should be shot.

'When they knew they were going to die, they were so calm', the man told his friend. 'They just said, "All right!" and asked for a little time to read their Book and pray. They weren't afraid.' Then he added, 'They were good. They were good people.'

This unexpected and unconfirmed report of their death had not been welcome because it came just about the time when the semi-official rumour that Minka and Margaret had been seen alive and well had revived hope. But there had been something about it that had the ring of truth, and when, a couple of weeks later, John Toop and Russell Gray saw for themselves the remains that had been so remarkably found in the jungle, saw the evidence that a bullet had passed through the back of each head, they believed. What they saw with their own eyes bore out so perfectly what they had heard a fortnight before, that they could doubt no more.

'It gives us such a thrill of pride to think that at the end, facing certain death, their witness was such that this Muslim remembered them as "good people",' said John later, reporting the incident. And when, the police investigations completed and the forensic experts satisfied, the funeral service was held on May 11th 1975 at Saiburi, the sorrow and the pathos were completely submerged by the rising notes of triumph. Hundreds of onlookers were gathered at the gates of the hospital, while inside the grounds were assembled the Thai officials and the ambassadors, the hospital staff and the missionaries, and the Thai and Malay Christians from far and near who had come to pay their tribute of love and respect to the two women who had lived, served, and died among them.

'We all came prepared to do this', Denis Lane, Overseas Director from Singapore, explained. The members of OMF had come to Thailand to share the sorrows as well as the joys, the lives and if need be the deaths of the people to whom God had sent them. Their Master had set that example. It was to Minka and Margaret that the privilege of demonstrating the sincerity of that committal had been given.

In many ways it was a very unusual ceremony. It is not the practice in Thailand to sing joyfully at funerals, to assert with conviction that death for the believer in Christ has already lost its sting, to lay emphasis on the certainty of resurrection. The distinguished visitors must have been rather surprised, too, that one of the speakers should be an inconspicuous young Thai villager who had been found by the nurses, he said, pain-ridden with leprosy and wanting to die. 'I was frightened of my disease, of the spirits, of death, but most of all of sin. It was Margaret

Morgan who showed me that Jesus had delivered me from the power of all these, and I "passed from death to life."

'When we heard that Minka and Margaret had been kidnapped', Jit continued, 'My friend Chern and I tried to offer ourselves in exchange. We knew the hardships they had endured in order to treat us, and we would have died for them gladly. We were worried, too, about the other leprosy patients left with no one to look after them . . . But God allowed Minka and Margaret to die, and wanted us to live. Now I don't want to live any more for myself, but for Him . . .' Still clutching the paper on which his speech had been carefully written, he retreated from the microphone and took his seat again.

Equally moving, and in some ways even more surprising, was the appearance of a Malay on the platform. There was a stir and a quickening of interest among the Muslims standing a distance away, but well within sound of the microphone as he started to speak. He too had been a leprosy patient, and had gone to the clinic in Pujud, from where the nurses had been kidnapped.

'But as a Muslim I had no desire to learn about Christ. All I cared about was getting well and being able to support my wife and children.' Then Uncle Mat, for it was he, went on to tell of the occasion when Minka treated the ulcer on his foot, how his resistance to the Lord crumbled at that moment and how, some months later, he became a Christian. His head held high, conscious of what the open affirmation of faith might bring to him in the way of hostility, even danger, he continued,

'Now, together with my wife, I serve as caretaker at the Malay Centre in Saiburi. We know this is where God wants us and that we must carry on Mother Minka's work—that of introducing Malay Muslims to the Lord Jesus.'

Perhaps that bold announcement did more than anything else to demonstrate to all that a Malay church had been firmly planted in south Thailand.

'It didn't pass unnoticed, you can be sure,' said Brenda two or three years later. She was in London, preparing to return again to south Thailand, and was sharing her reminiscences with a friend, reliving those unforgettable days. 'Uncle Mat received a number of threatening letters after the funeral, and he wasn't the only one. Some of the other Malay Christians have had them, too.'

'But they've stood firm?' she was asked.

'Yes', she said. 'They've stood firm.'

When the Apostle Paul wrote to the Philippians from a Roman jail, he declared categorically that what had happened to him, so far from hindering, had actually advanced the Gospel. The believers, knowing of his sufferings for Christ's sake, had taken courage themselves, and become bolder in their own witness. Nearly two thousand years later the same principle was at work in south Thailand. The death of Minka and Margaret on that lonely hillside in the jungle was still having its indefinable influence on the lives of those in whose service the sacrifice had been made. The quality of discipleship had been deepened.

One way in which it manifested itself was in the willingness of Malay believers to use their voices in making Christian programmes for cassette recordings. This had proved to be one of the most effective means of proclaiming the Gospel in the clinics, but in the early days the difficulty had been the reluctance of any Malays to have their voices recorded for this purpose. They were afraid of the indignation of the Muslims, and what that might lead to. Now, however, local Malay Christians were willing to have their voices recorded, even though they knew they would be recognised.

The work of producing the New Testament in the local Malay dialect, too, had gone steadily forward because now there were two Malay believers ready to help with the translating. 'Both were contacted and treated for years in the Pujud clinic', Brenda said. 'After Minka and Margaret were captured, however, the clinic there was never re-opened. The landlord was afraid to let us rent the place after that. The patients who were attending there had to go to Pattani instead.'

So it had come about that by 1977 the little home in which Minka and Margaret lived had become the biggest leprosy clinic in south Thailand. From far and wide the patients came, Thai, Chinese, but mainly Malays, entering by the little room where the two nurses used to have their daily devotions, going through to what was once the reception room where Jit sat taking skin smears for the pathology laboratory examinations, or helping with the treatment of ulcers.

Every Sunday a worship service was held under the car port. Those who gathered for it were Malays, among them those who openly acknowledged that they were now Christians . . .

One day, shortly after it became known how Minka and Margaret had died, Fiona Lindsay was in the Malay Centre at Saiburi, trying to teach Christian truths to the handful of Malays gathered there. Her knowledge of their language was limited, so she had taken along something with which they were very familiar, as an object lesson. It was a stalk of rice. She held it up for them to see, then asked,

'What must happen before we can get more rice?'

'The grains must be planted in the ground', was the answer.

'What then?'

'New stalks come up, more rice grains grow . . .'

'But what happens to the rice grains that were planted?'

There was a rather mystified silence. Then someone said, 'They disintegrate.'

Fiona nodded eagerly. This was what she had wanted. 'There's a verse in John's Gospel we haven't translated yet', she said. 'We didn't know what words to use, but now you've given them to us.' Then she translated, as best she could, the passage she knew so well. *Except a corn of wheat fall into the ground and die, it abides alone. But if it die, it brings forth much fruit.* All eyes were on her as she continued in a voice charged with emotion,

'That's what's happened to Minka and Margaret.'

There was a deep stillness in the little room. Fiona looked into their faces, and knew they had understood.

The Malay Christians in south Thailand often sing a song now which is peculiarly their own. With Fiona's help, Uncle Mat composed it.

> A seed of rice, one grain,
>   Cannot become a lot
> Unless it is planted in the ground
>   And there disintegrates.
>
> Then only can it sprout
>   And bring forth many grains,
> We men are like that, too,
>   We men are like that, too.
>
> The one who clings to life
>   Who counts his own life dear,
> Cannot receive new life from God
>   He always stays alone.
>
> But he who will not love
>   Or count his own life dear
> That man will get new life from God
>   And live for evermore.